UNDER TIN ROOFS
CAYMAN IN THE 1920s

BY

AARONA BOOKER KOHLMAN

FOREWORD BY
H. G. NOWAK (THE BAREFOOT MAN)

Published by
The Cayman Islands National Museum
P. O. Box 2189 GT
Grand Cayman
Cayman Islands

Photographs: N. L. Booker
Illustrations and cover design: Wray Banker
Typeset: Dace McCoy Ground
Pre-Press: Cayman Free Press Ltd.

ISBN 976-8104-73-2

Printed and bound by Limited Run Publishing Solutions, USA

All incidents described in this book are real. In some cases, typical Caymanian names have been substituted for the actual names of the individuals involved.

To my mother and father

To my husband, Leslie,
and children,
Fay, David, Kathleen, Richard, Linda

Acknowledgements

I extend my sincerest thanks to all of those who have helped me in the writing of these memoirs. First of all, I thank George Nowak (The Barefoot Man), who first suggested the project and gave me valuable advice in the beginning stages. Anita Ebanks, Director of the Cayman Islands National Museum, whom I have known since she was a child, has carried through the publication, and I thank her for her kindness, patience and assistance. I am deeply grateful for editorial suggestions and guidance from Dr. Philip Pedley, Director of the Cayman Islands National Archive, who furnished the critical eye I had been looking for. Michael Hislop shared his first-hand knowledge in preparing the Glossary, Bill Tennent shared in the preparation for publication, and Wray Banker is responsible for the beautiful and appropriate artwork. Good friends Ella Hurlston Latter, Elizabeth Hutchings Hurlston and Georgette Hurlston Ebanks read the manuscript and I am grateful for their help. Many others have helped me in various ways, and they are too numerous to mention individually.

Of course, my deepest gratitude goes to my husband, who has given me his full support and help, and to my children who have also given their encouragement.

Finally, I must thank my parents, who made it all possible by taking me to Cayman in the first place, and all my cherished friends, who shared my experiences and live on in my memories.

Aarona Booker Kohlman
Lamoni, Iowa

Contents

Foreword

I am often accused of living in the past . . . well, it is a valid accusation. I'm the one who doesn't like things as they are . . . I like them as they were. I'm sorry, but in my opinion tropical islands should not consist of satellite dishes, traffic jams and fast food outlets. Though I've been lucky enough to prosper with this little island's prosperity and I hate to sound like a cynic, I would gladly turn back the hands of time if some magical genie granted me such a wish. I would do this not to seek my youth, but to once again live on that placid sun drenched island bursting with charm and tranquility.

You see, I remember George Town when goats grazed in the spot where our present Courthouse and Legislative building now sit . . . I remember the ships unloading giant turtles for market at the same spot where now ultra-modern cruise ships unload visitors by the thousands. Some of these visitors buy souvenirs in a gift shop along the harbour — the same shop was once a small store selling everything from salt fish to bananas. And believe it or not, I can remember when we had only half a dozen taxi drivers on our little island. Now, if my memories from only a few decades ago sound delightful . . . well, what about the recollections of Aarona Kohlman? Aarona was but 12 years old when she arrived here on the sailing schooner *Lady Antoinette* in 1925. Her father, N. L. Booker, a missionary, had in his possession something few people back then had the luxury of owning on Grand Cayman. No, I'm not talking about the Bible . . . Bibles were plentiful: I'm talking about a camera. Can you imagine the expression on some of the old-timers' faces when Mr. Booker would point a camera in their direction and then try to explain that he had just captured the moment on film? Aarona Kohlman needs not to imagine, she was there and her recollection of such times is as crystal clear as the sea that surrounds us.

It was almost a decade ago when I first saw her collection of photos. I was not only impressed, I was puzzled . . . puzzled as to why she was carting around these time capsules (rare photos in a shoe box, to be exact.)

While I awed at her photo collection and queried "Who's that? What's this? Where was this taken?" Aarona reminisced . . . she is a fountain of knowledge on the days gone by. A time when shopping trips consisted of a two day voyage aboard a sailing vessel to Kingston, Jamaica, instead of an hour's jet ride to the malls of Miami. A time when mosquitoes were so thick they killed cattle and a time when the valuable real estate along the

Seven Mile Beach was but a collection of cockspurs, cocoplums, seagrape and casuarina trees . . . the word condominium had not even been introduced into the English language.

I've always felt her memoirs and photos should be published. In fact, at one time I was going to handle the whole project myself. Well, my tours, family and song writing got in the way. The 90's bring good news . . . Anita Ebanks felt as strongly about this project as I did, and as she is Director of the Cayman Islands National Museum, Aarona's book could not have been placed into better hands.

Caymanians will delight at the following pages. They will know that her stories are not tales of fantasy. The visitors reading this book will find it hard to believe that there was such a time on an island that is now home to over 500 banks and probably double that number of taxi drivers.

This is a book about a past that will never be recovered, events that will never be recaptured, innocence and charm that faded from our shores the moment developers laid eyes on the beautiful Cayman Islands.

 H. G. Nowak (The Barefoot Man)
Breakers, 1993

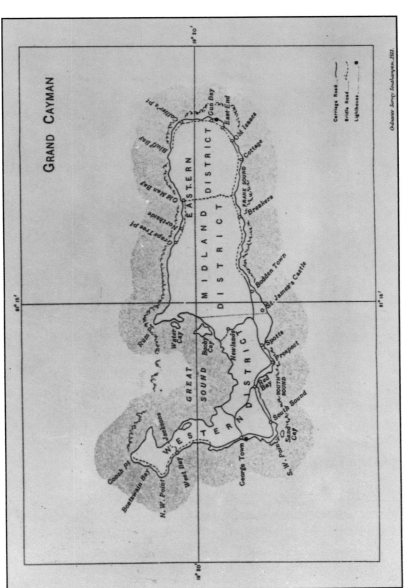

This 1913 map of Grand Cayman shows the main communities and roads that existed when the Booker family arrived in 1925. The unchanging nature of the island is reflected in the fact that the same map was published in Colonial Reports for several decades.

Introduction

When I was twelve years old, my family moved from the United States to Grand Cayman. My father was a missionary for the Reorganized Church of Jesus Christ of Latter Day Saints, and we moved often. Until after my marriage, I lived in Grand Cayman longer than in any other place. Furthermore, we lived there during my adolescent years, a period when one makes lasting friends and forms enduring memories. My father and another missionary, J. Charles May, spent six months in the Isle of Pines and Cayman in 1924. I was delighted when the church appointed him to return with his family for an extended time. We arrived in Cayman in November, 1925.

It was an enchanted time for me, when I was free to come and go with new-found friends, swimming, bicycling up and down the winding roads, picking mangoes and orchids, going in the sea, horse-back riding on Diablo (Farrell Jackson's horse), learning to thatch a roof, collecting shells, sailing in the moonlight, finding lobsters in North Sound, and experiencing my first "puppy love."

Memories, though vivid, can sometimes be different from reality. So I have checked facts with other people and with written records, such as my own diaries and the Cayman Islands Annual Colonial Reports. Nevertheless, some incidents I clearly remember seem to have slipped from the recollection of others. If the reader remembers something differently, let it be no reflection on either of us. This is the way I remember it.

The pictures illustrating this account were taken by my father. He developed and printed them, although he knew nothing about photographic processing before reaching Cayman. He sent to Eastman Kodak for directions and chemicals and learned by trial and error. It seems remarkable to me that they have survived, without any special care, all these years.

There are a few pictures, however, that someone else took, because he also developed photographs for others, and often saved a copy of some picture he wanted for himself. He did all the developing and printing in a make-shift laboratory with no running water or electricity. When we left the island, he turned all his equipment over to Otto and Ella Hurlston and instructed them in its use.

I often go back in memory to my adolesent days in Grand Cayman, and as I continue to visit the Island and my many friends, my memories endure in the midst of the changes. Memories are precious and personal, very personal. Someone else will have memories different from mine, but I am here sharing my memories of Cayman. I hope they will help others to understand more clearly what Cayman was like in the 1920s.

Aarona Booker Kohlman
Lamoni, Iowa

Crewmen on the lookout for a fresh meal?

CHAPTER 1

Cayman Bound

T he *Lady Antoinette* rose . . . and fell . . . rose . . . and fell . . . rose . . . and fell, as she sailed down Tampa Bay in the early afternoon of October 19, 1925. Literally wiggling with excitement, I sat on the top of the cabin, dangling my legs. My mother and father and I were at last actually setting out on our journey to the West Indies. I was twelve years old, and ever since my father, a missionary, had spent six months on the Isle of Pines and Grand Cayman a year before, I had searched every night possible for the first star, repeating fervently, "Starlight, starbright, First star I see tonight, I wish I may, I wish I might, Have the wish I wish tonight," and then wishing that I could go to Cayman.

My excitement was heightened by the repeated delays in starting the voyage. We had spent a couple of weeks near Tampa with good friends, Mom and Pap Chevalier and their children. Our plan was to take a steamship to Havana, Cuba, go across Cuba by train, and take a smaller steamer from Batabano to the Isle of Pines. After a short stay there, we would get passage on a Caymanian schooner to Grand Cayman. However, after only a few days in Tampa, my father was called back to Mobile, Alabama, by the death of his father. When he returned, he began to investigate finding passage to Cuba, but discovered that the *Lady Antoinette* was in port, and would be sailing for Cayman via the Isle of Pines in a few days. Furthermore, we could secure passage for only $15 each, which was less for the three of us than for one of us going through Havana. Daddy had returned to the States on the *Antoinette* the year before and he assured us it wasn't too bad.

So passage was engaged, and we were told that the ship would be sailing Thursday of the next week. Then we got a call saying the little auxiliary engine needed some work done on it, that it would be Friday or Saturday before we could sail. We finally received word that we would set out at noon on Saturday.

Mom, Pap, Edgar, Arthur, Catherine, and Lois were all up to eat a hearty breakfast with us. By nine o'clock we loaded our suitcases and boxes in the car, they bid us a tearful goodbye, and with Arthur at the wheel, we headed for the docks. Very few Americans had even heard of the Isle of Pines, and even fewer knew of the existence of the Cayman Islands.

Mother's kerosene cooking stove and Singer sewing machine and two or three boxes of household goods had been taken to the ship several days before, and by ten Saturday morning, we caught sight for the first time of our little 70-foot Cayman-built, two-masted schooner. A number of Caymanian seamen were working around the dock, slowly loading the ship under the direction of Captain Tom Jackson. I was in a fever to get aboard, but Cap'n Tom told us "We not goin' cast off 'til about two o'clock."

We told Arthur goodbye, and wandered off to kill time for three or four hours around the waterfront. After hot dogs and root beer (at 5¢ each!), we were back at shipside well before two o'clock, waiting for the word to get aboard. There wasn't much to see or do, and we had very little money — none to waste on non-essentials — so how we spent the time remains a blur in my memory. The hour arrived, and we were told that the engine still wasn't repaired, and to come back at 11 o'clock Sunday.

The Chevaliers lived some distance from the city, two miles from the end of the streetcar line, and worked long hours in their truck garden. Daddy, although reluctant to bother them, called, and made arrangements for Arthur to meet us at Sulphur Springs, the end of the line, when he could quit work. Tired and disappointed, we spent the night with our friends. My parents arranged for some other friends to pick us up Sunday morning to take us to the boat.

The goodbyes second time around the next morning were not nearly as tearful nor emotional as the first ones, but still were fervent, and back we went to the pier. No need for details — again our departure was delayed two or three times. When evening approached, we were told once more of a delay — we would not sail until the next morning. We couldn't face another farewell scene with the Chevalier family. I declared, "I'll do most anything to keep from telling them good-bye again. I can't do that another time." My parents were of the same opinion, so somehow they found an inexpensive, dingy room near the pier where we could spend the night. By that time my faith in the power of the first star was a little shaken.

We whiled away the next morning, responding to announcements of imminent departure with skepticism, but about one o'clock, to our immense relief, we were told, "Unna get aboard." The engine was in working order, and apparently no one could think of another reason to delay departure; the lines were cast off, Rudy, the engineer, started the little gasoline engine, and the seamen hoisted the sails. Our ship was under way. I was disappointed that there was no friend to witness the start of our great adventure. I remarked wistfully, "It doesn't seem one bit as if we are going away off when there isn't a single person here to tell us good-bye and wave to us as we sail away."

In the following years, we discovered that such delay was not at all uncommon. In fact, sailing at the time first announced was almost unheard of!

"This is fun!" I proclaimed as we came to the top of a swell and began the glide to the bottom, and on up again. It was something like a slow-motion roller coaster, but at that point anything that involved our moving away from land would have been fun. In my new khaki knickers, which had just come

Mealtime for those passengers well enough to eat!

into style for girls, my matching shirt, and brown oxfords that catered to my tomboy nature, I was off on a journey to the Unknown. (My mother, not realizing she was being daring, had also chosen knickers as the most sensible attire for the journey.)

Suddenly, in spite of the cool stiff wind, I began to feel very hot, and sweat popped out all over me. "My, it's getting hot," I observed. Daddy looked at me with a little smile, but said nothing. After a few moments, as I got hotter and hotter, I repeated my remark, then suddenly forgot about how much fun I was having when I realized that I'd better head for the rail

— FAST! I made it just in time, too miserable to even resent my Dad's chuckling.

Mother was already below in the double bunk she and I were to share; she had not for a moment thought that we were having fun. Poor Mother! On all sea trips, no matter how calm the sea, she spent most of the time in her bunk, seasick. Daddy had a single bunk crossway of the cabin, above the low door that gave entry to the small engine room. Every time Rudy opened the door, a cloud of gasoline fumes swirled in to emphasize the constant hot oil odor of the engine, which seeped around and through the thin wooden door. The *Antoinette* had been built as a "windjammer" with no place for an engine. Later a small engine room had been built in the hold, adjoining the cabin. The only means of entering it was through one small door into the cabin. This proximity added the vibrations of the engine to the rolling and pitching of the ship. The small cabin had five or six bunks. Besides the three of us, there were a Cayman woman and her three children and five or six men. Those without a bunk stretched out on the floor in the center of the cabin. Anyone needing to cross the cabin had to step over them, and if the boat lurched, stepped on them.

Most of the passengers were sick, and had no desire for food, but the children never missed a meal — regularly the food went down, and just as regularly it came up again. One corner of the cabin was walled off to make a small closet, containing nothing but a bucket for a toilet. Usually — unfortunately not always — those who were sick managed to make it to the bucket if they didn't have time to get to the rail. Several times a day a seaman would pick his way over and around the children on the floor and lug the odoriferous bucket on deck to empty it over the rail.

I remember often waking in the middle of the night, stifling in the smelly, stuffy cabin, wanting to go on deck for fresh air. We slept in our clothes, of course, and I would make my way over the sleeping children and up the companionway to the deck, which was covered with kegs of nails, leaving only a few bare spots so the seamen could do their work. I would sit on a keg, hunched over, with the boat rolling and the sea water sloshing over my bare feet. I slumped there until I vomited over the rail, then made my way back down to my bunk.

It is no wonder that the passengers were seasick; in addition to the gasoline fumes and the normal musty, wet-wood, sour odor of a schooner, another odor assaulted us from the full load of commercial fertilizer, which may smell better than nature's own from the barnyard, but not much. Then there was the odor of onions, fresh fish or canned salmon, and other food

Bringing passengers and cargo ashore in Hog Stye Bay

cooking, and tobacco smoke.

By Thursday, when the sea had calmed and we were just off Cape Antonio, Cuba, I got my "sea legs" and was no longer sick. (I found on subsequent voyages that I got over seasickness after three or four days.) But even before that, I don't remember ever wishing my dream had not come true. I was living adventure such as I'd only dreamed of before.

We left the *Lady Antoinette* when we reached Nueva Gerona, capital of the Isle of Pines (Isla de Piños), which lies southwest of the west end of Cuba, and which belongs to Cuba. When we stepped ashore, to my surprise it wasn't solid ground; at least, it didn't feel like solid ground. The ground seemed to be rolling just as the deck had done, and we lurched our way through the sleepy little town to our dwelling, across from a small park-like square and the Ayuntamiento (city hall), with people staring and laughing at the women in pants.

We spent about six weeks in Nueva Gerona in a high-ceilinged dwelling whose massive wooden door opened directly onto the sidewalk. I was fascinated by the beautiful tile floors and the iron bars at all the windows. We drew water from a well in the backyard shared with several other dwellings, and shared the outhouse also. Our drinking water was purchased from Mr. Henri Reever, a Canadian and a member of our church, who drove his horse and wagon, loaded with huge casks of water, through the streets of the town. We kept the water in a large pottery jar on a stand in the kitchen. Our time in Gerona was filled with new sights, sounds and experiences, and I was a little sad when the time came to move on to our more permanent home in Cayman.

Once more we gathered our belongings and embarked on the *Lady Antoinette* to complete our journey. Once more Mother took to her bunk seasick, and I, too, was queasy, but not as sick as she. However, the voyage was not nearly as long, and we were delighted when land was sighted in a couple of days.

It was dark by the time we anchored in Hog Stye Bay. It was not possible to tie up to a dock, so we clambered into the small boat to be rowed ashore. My father had notified our church members that we would be coming on the *Antoinette,* and it seemed to us that the entire population of George Town was crowded on the rocks to see Brother Booker again and to see what his wife and daughter looked like. Many willing hands helped us with our luggage, and dozens of people escorted us the short distance to our house, next to Merrens' store on Shedden Road. Everybody was talking at once, it seemed, and for the first time I felt a little forlorn and homesick.

I had known I would not understand Spanish in Nueva Gerona, but Caymanians were supposed to speak English — and I could understand scarcely a word anyone said! Furthermore, I was hungry, for we had not eaten on the *Antoinette* before coming ashore, and as it was eight or nine o'clock, no one thought to offer us any food.

Finally, our welcoming party left for their homes, one by one, and we crawled into our beds, too tired and too happy to be "home" at last to notice our hunger pangs.

My wish-on-a-star had actually come true, and we were launched into our new life.

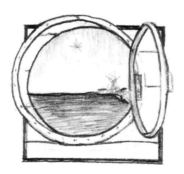

Bodden Town houses featured a variety of roof materials and architectural styles.

CHAPTER 2

Under the House Tops

Merrendale, the home of H. O. Merren Sr. and his family, was where I spent many happy hours with the Merren children. Merrendale was typical of the homes of the wealthier Caymanians, and I remember this type of home only in the George Town area. Merrendale was a two-storey, white, frame house, with a veranda across the front of both stories. An outside staircase at the front of the house ran up to the second storey, which contained the living room and bedrooms and a wide hall. The kitchen and dining room, one or two bedrooms, a small room for live-in maids, and a real bathroom occupied the ground floor. An inside staircase also led up to the second floor. Merrendale, and other houses of its type, had screened glass windows, with heavy wooden shutters to be closed when a storm or hurricane threatened. Ceilings were high, making the rooms airy and cool. The hardwood floors were dyed with red ochre or red mangrove, and waxed by women on hands and knees. Wax cakes were rubbed over the boards by hand, then the floor was polished with a brush made by sawing off the end of a dry coconut husk, the stiff fibers serving as bristles. I had not had experience with waxed floors before, and I loved to walk barefoot on the smooth, cool boards.

Our first home, next to Merrens' store and just off the waterfront of Hog Stye Bay, was typical of the more numerous one-storey frame houses, usually painted white, often trimmed in bright colors (especially in the districts of East End, North Side, and West Bay), and with corrugated tin "house tops." (My bedroom had no ceiling, and I liked to lie in bed at night listening to the pounding of the rain on the tin roof.) These houses were decorated along the ridge of the roof and around the eaves with gingerbread scrolls. Although our house had two bay windows and only a small entry porch, most houses of this type had a porch across the front, with a fancy, scrolled railing. There were usually four or five rooms, and sometimes a kitchen and dining room such as ours, but some also still had a detached kitchen. Our second

A traditional "cookrum" (cookroom/kitchen) made of wattle walls and a thatch roof.

home, McCoy's Villa, was an example of this type of house.

When we visited districts away from George Town, we stayed with families who lived in the more numerous, smaller one-storey houses made of "lime" (a kind of concrete) which were white-washed regularly, keeping them sparkling white. (Some smaller homes were frame, usually painted white.) Thatch house tops had been common, but by the time we arrived on the island, most of these had corrugated tin roofs. The kitchens of these two or three room houses were smaller structures, sometimes just open sheds, which sat a few yards from the house, where the cooking was done in a "cookrum" (cookroom) over an open fire on a raised platform, called the caboose. A few families had, however, moved up to kerosene stoves.

Most of these houses did not have ceilings, the single-board partitions going up to the rafters, allowing better circulation. These houses also had the typical waxed hardwood floors. Many of them did not have glass windows nor screens, but had only the heavy wooden shutters, which were open in the daytime and closed at night or in rainy weather. (Some Caymanians, like other West Indians, thought that night air was unhealthful, to be avoided if possible.)

A few very modest, one-room houses, some frame, some "lime", were found around the island, but these, too, were usually kept whitewashed or painted, and the yards were neatly swept. Even fewer were the one-room wattle-and-daub houses with thatch house tops, some with dirt floors. (Thatch roofs were mostly used for sheds by this time. I learned to put on thatch at Farrel Jackson's place in Newlands when I helped Marvick Smith, who lived with them, thatch a shed. I'm sure I could still do it today.) It would have been very hard in those days to find a true shanty or hovel; even though some people were very poor, they kept their houses and yards neat and clean.

When a hurricane threatened, people rushed to secure their homes as much as possible. With no radio or other means of communication with other parts of the world, the local weather experts depended on their own wits, intuition, knowledge, and the barometer to forecast a hurricane, but its speed, location, and direction were purely speculative. When the first warning of a storm was sounded, all shutters were nailed shut, and thatch roofs were somewhat protected by stringing two or three ropes across the top of the house, wrapped around small logs that stretched across each side of the roof. The ends of the rope on each side were tied firmly to two-by-fours or small logs which lay on the ground. Everything was left in place until the threat of the hurricane seemed to be gone.

All homes had to supply their own water and sanitary facilities. Merrendale was the only home I was ever in with a Delco plant to supply electricity for pumping water from an elevated tank-cistern in the backyard for the indoor stool and shower. (The outdoor privy remained just in case.) We kids thought it a great treat to be invited to use the shower to rinse off the salt water after going in the sea.

All but the smallest homes had a "bath" room which was just that — a room for taking baths in a galvanized wash tub. Caymanians were very clean people in spite of the lack of modern conveniences such as running water. Some homes in the bush had no outhouses; one had to go into the bush, a most uncomfortable business in mosquito or tick season.

In the mosquito season, a smoke pot was a necessary piece of equipment for a trip to the outhouse or the bush. During the tick season, if we were staying in Newlands, when we came back from the bush we had to thoroughly examine ourselves and each other for ticks, dropping those we picked off into the chimney of a kerosene lamp to burn them. (That produced an odor never to be forgotten.)

All homes, except those with thatch roofs, had cisterns in the yard near the house, or oil drums, for catching water collected by gutters around the eaves. People without cisterns could usually catch enough water to get by, but in a drought they would have to carry water from a neighbor's cistern. The only wells were shallow with brackish water unfit for drinking.

Some families made arrangements with others who had large cisterns to get water, which they had to carry home in buckets. The usual arrangement was that the users would help the cistern owner to clean the cistern when it needed to be done. This was no small job.

We had a very large cistern at McCoy's Villa. My father consulted the experts on the best time to clean our cistern — just before the rainy season, he was told. When Cleavy announced that the time had come, he and others who used the cistern came to help. In a few hours the cistern was empty, and it was thoroughly scrubbed and cleaned.

In a few days all the water we had stored was gone, but the rain had not come. I remember carrying buckets of water from Petra (now Grand Old House) for about a week before the rainy season began and the cistern began to fill. That was real training in water conservation.

Our first home in Cayman, in the center of George Town, which we rented from Merrens, had a very small room little larger than a closet, between the kitchen and dining room, that was the bathroom. It contained only a standard claw-footed bathtub, which had to be filled by carrying water

Hilda Christian, laundress hired by the Bookers.

from the cistern, and which was drained through a hole in the floor.

Our next home, McCoy's Villa, also owned by Merrens, was much grander, to my way of thinking. There were porches across the front and one side, and a back porch with a swing as well. Not only was it larger and better furnished, but the bath room was quite large, and had a lavatory with working faucets and a shower over a large, oval, galvanized tub. Beside the tub was a trap door in the floor; after a shower, the trap door was opened, and the tub tipped over to let the water pour onto the sand below. We even had warm water any time after about noon. It was my job to pump water from the cistern to the oil drum on the roof each morning. The heat of the sun soon warmed it.

In this room my father rigged up a primitive darkroom in which he developed and printed pictures, using a kerosene lamp or daylight to make the prints, counting to determine the exposure time. If the print was too dark, he did another with a lower count; if too light, a longer count. The prints were hung to dry on a line strung across the room.

Washing clothes was hard labor: scrubbing the clothes on a washboard in a galvanized tub set up on a bench in the yard using strong yellow soap. The brackish water from wells could be used for laundry. The clothes had to be wrung by hand, of course. White clothes and bedding were spread out on the sand to be bleached by the sun. Women usually ironed in the yard with flat irons heated over charcoal, on makeshift ironing boards. Mother had never been one to do laundry on a washboard, and in any case we didn't have tubs and a washboard, so she hired Hilda and Louise, from an area of the town known as "Maryland", to do our washing. Every Monday, both of them would walk two or three miles to our house, stop and visit awhile, then carry the dirty laundry back home. Unless rain delayed them, they brought everything back in two days' time, washed and starched and ironed. For this service, they asked only three shillings, but my parents insisted on giving them five shillings. My mother justified this extravagance by the fact that they needed the money very badly, as neither one had a husband nor other family to provide for them.

In the early days — until the 1900's — most furniture had been made on the island, usually of mahogany or other local hardwoods. Canopied four-poster beds with hand-carved posts were common — too common, for by the 1920's, mail order had come to Cayman, and everyone wanted an iron bedstead from Sears Roebuck. The "common" four-posters were cut up for firewood or thrown out in the yard. My mother could have had such a bed in trade for a cheap mail order bedstead, but she simply didn't have the money to buy a bed and ship it home. We had to be satisfied with enjoying the beautiful four-posters with flowered and beribboned canopies in McCoy's Villa.

One standard item of furniture has always been the hammock. No matter how small the house, it contained at least one hammock, strung from one corner of a room to another corner. The larger the house, the more hammocks. A house with a porch usually had a swing, and yard swings were frequently seen, too.

A common sight until recent years was a house in progress. Caymanians did not go into debt to build a house. The husband would go to sea or overseas to work, and save money for a house. He would come home for a few months and build as much of the house as he had money to pay for. He would repeat this process until he eventually got it to the place where the family could move in, and still later the house would be finished. Because things grow so rapidly in the tropics, a stranger would have marvelled at how many "abandoned" houses, over-grown with weeds and shrubs, were around the island. But if he had come back five years later, he would have seen that they had not been abandoned at all, but were finished and occupied.

Caymanians loved their homes, and kept house and yard neat and clean, even if modest. All houses were either painted or whitewashed, and kept in good repair. They were neat and uncluttered inside as well, reflecting the peaceful, quiet, hospitable nature of the people. The door was always open in welcome to friend or stranger.

Butchering turtle below the market at Hog Stye Bay.

CHAPTER 3

Our Daily Breadkind

Eziethamae Rankine, fifteen years old in 1925, already had a full set of dentures. Loss of teeth at a very early age was not uncommon in Cayman at that time. A diet heavy in sugar and starch, and deficient in calcium and fresh vegetables, caused the early decay and loss of teeth in the days before modern shipping brought all kinds of food into Cayman. I later realized that one balancing factor in early day nutrition, however, was the abundance of sea food and citrus fruits, which provided many of the necessary minerals and vitamins.

My mother was very interested in and knowledgeable about proper nutrition, and she had grown up on a farm. She was convinced that vegetables would grow on the island, but Caymanians were sure they wouldn't. As the only way to import food was by a Cayman schooner, without refrigeration, fresh vegetables such as beans, peas, tomatoes, cucumbers, celery, lettuce, cabbage, etc., were unknown. The only vegetables we could get were those that could be shipped in cans.

Aware of our plight from my mother's letters, our truck gardener friends, the Chevaliers in Tampa, sometimes sent us a crate of vegetables on the *Antoinette*. Almost half of the produce would be rotten by the time it reached us, but Mother would salvage what she could, and we thoroughly enjoyed the "fresh" vegetables. Daddy finally tried planting vegetables in our sandy back yard at McCoy's Villa. He had three tomato plants, six lettuces, and three dozen stalks of corn. We almost drooled over corn on the cob. Caymanians grew corn, but let it mature, then hung the ears from the rafters in the house to dry. Before it could be used, it had to be soaked and grated.

My parents had some cucumber seeds sent down which they persuaded Leighton Bush to plant. One vine alone produced nearly one hundred cucumbers, but even this did not really convince anyone that vegetables could be grown successfully.

No eggs were imported, and as the local hens had to forage for most of their own food, eggs were not plentiful. Neither do I remember ever eating chicken.

The only meats available were turtle or beef, and occasionally pork, but fish, lobsters, conch, and whelks were plentiful, as well as land crabs in season, and were available for the catching, or if they had to be bought, they were very inexpensive. Because there was no refrigeration available, everything had to be cooked and eaten promptly, and reheated thoroughly if kept over after a meal.

In the 1920's, a small ice-making machine run by a generator was in operation at the ice cream parlor, managed by Miss Lulu Bodden, on the waterfront in George Town. At top capacity and when it could be kept running, it produced no more than about five hundred pounds of ice every two or three days, in one hundred pound blocks. Consequently no one customer was allowed to buy more than two or three pounds, unless he reserved it ahead of time for making ice cream for a "cake sale." Ice was expensive — it cost two pence for a small chunk, about a pound, when in the States ten cents (equivalent to five pence) would buy 25 pounds. My father would buy one or two pounds of ice to use when he was developing and printing pictures, and Mother and I would usually manage to scrounge enough for a little limeade, and how good it tasted!

Cows were butchered every Saturday, early in the morning, and the meat was sold that day. In places such as Savannah, butchering was done under a big mango tree by the roadside, and the carcass was hung from a limb. In George Town, the market sat on the rocks by Hog Stye Bay, so that all the refuse could be dumped in the sea. This practice, of course, attracted sharks, so although Hog Stye Bay was a popular swimming place for my friends and me, we did not go in the sea at that spot on Saturdays.

Meat was not sold in cuts such as steaks or roasts, but was hacked off in chunks from any part of the carcass. Whatever cuts you got cost six pence a pound. The butcher poked a hole through each piece with a machete or a knife, and strung the pieces on a length of thatch, knotting the ends together so the bundle could be carried easily. We once saw a man on horseback with his bundle of meat tied to the back of his saddle, riding home with the chunks slapping against the horse's sweaty rump in the blazing sun. The usual method of cooking beef was to make it into a stew, with hot peppers and "breadkind".

Turtle meat was a welcome change in diet, but as turtles were no longer found around Cayman, they were brought back on the deck of schooners from the turtling grounds off the coast of Central America. The huge creatures, green turtle weighing up to 400 pounds and hawksbill up to 200 pounds, were transported on their backs. They could live two or three weeks out of water if they were kept cool by having sea water sloshed over them

Bringing provisions to market?

occasionally. However, when the ship was in the process of catching the turtles, or when they were awaiting slaughter, they were confined in a "crawl" — a pen constructed of long poles in shallow water among the mangroves along the shore. In Cayman these were found in North Sound.

Turtle was butchered almost anywhere outdoors, often on the waterfront, and sold on the spot. Turtle, like beef, was usually stewed, although I do remember having turtle steak a few times. For Caymanians a sickly-green layer of fatty gristle just beneath the skin was the choicest part. Although I liked almost every other Caymanian food, I ate that with great difficulty. Fish was sometimes fried, but also often stewed or made into fish soup. Coconut milk, squeezed by hand from dry coconut grated on a homemade tin grater, was used in all kinds of stew — except turtle stew.

"Breadkind" was the staple of a true Cayman diet, and included cassava, yam (not a sweet potato), coco (looking somewhat like yam), breadfruit, sweet potatoes — all of them starchy. Only native-grown fruits were available, but were plentiful in their seasons — mangoes, guavas, star apples, guineps, naseberries (sapodillas), sweet and sour sops, papayas, avocados, limes, oranges, shaddocks (an early variety of grapefruit), sea grapes, tamarinds, wild plums, cocoplums, bananas, bottlers and plantains (cooking bananas), and coconuts.

Another staple was rice-and-peas ("peas" being red beans) cooked with coconut milk and hot peppers. This became one of our favorite foods. A true Caymanian "fast food" was the meat patty, pastry filled with highly seasoned ground beef. Conchs were made into stew, and also marinated raw, and whelks were another delicacy in stew. Land crabs which were very plentiful in their season, when they lived sheltered lives in the miles of rock fences that were then common, were also a favored food. They stayed hidden in the rocks during the day, but swarmed out at night when they could be picked up easily. Louise, who did our laundry, would reach into a hole in the rock wall and pull them out. I never had nerve enough to try that, even though she assured me there was no danger from their claws as they went into the holes "claws first." Crabs were so plentiful that the roads would be almost paved by those crushed by cars or other vehicles. Breadfruit salad, almost indistinguishable from potato salad, became another of our favorites. All these foods mentioned have been favorites through the years, with few changes in ingredients.

Because of the lack of refrigeration, the only butter or margarine that could be shipped in came in cans from Denmark. It had been treated for use in the tropics so that it would not liquefy in the heat. However, although it was soft enough to be liquid, it retained an unappetizing jelly-like appearance. It was also very expensive, so we used it very little. The scarcity of butter was a real hardship for Daddy and me. We liked butter and lots of it. It took us years to catch up on butter when we returned to the States.

Cows on the island had a hard time finding food, as grazing was meager and little if any cattle feed was imported. Consequently the little milk they produced was of a very poor quality (it required no processing to be skimmed milk), and had to be boiled to make it safe to drink. Mr. Leighton (Bush) produced the only milk I knew of that was rich enough to produce enough cream to make butter. Fresh milk was sold only privately, bottled in tall, green, liquor bottles with cork stoppers. Only evaporated or condensed milk was shipped in, as powdered milk was not yet known. Our family used a lot of evaporated milk; we even came to like it diluted for drinking, and we poured it undiluted on our cereal. (Boxed, ready-to-eat cereals were scarce and expensive. Because of the ever-warm weather, Mother didn't like to cook oatmeal nor did we want hot cereal, so we learned to eat rolled oats uncooked, with evaporated milk.)

Some white sugar was shipped in, but most of the sugar used was a raw brown sugar from Jamaica, very moist, with a pungent Jamaican molasses flavor, from which bits of trash had to be picked out. It gave an interesting flavor to limeade!

No bakery existed, so women made their own bread, as well as their own dry yeast cakes. Some women would occasionally sell a few loaves of bread. Mrs. Marie Bodden, a neighbor, kept Mother supplied with yeast cakes. Many women still cooked and baked on the open cooking platform filled with sand — the "caboose" — in a shed set away from the house. Some used wood stoves, and a very few enjoyed the modern convenience of a kerosene stove. My parents had very wisely brought a kerosene stove.

A favorite Cayman dessert has always been heavy cake, which is made from coconut milk, grated breadkind, and sugar — lots of sugar! It is very sweet and rich, stiffer than pudding but moister than cake. Sometimes it was cooked at night, after the day's other cooking was done, as it took several hours to cook. I remember sitting up late with Chrissie Watler and other girl friends at her home in Savannah while her mother, Aunt Jennie, baked heavy cake for Christmas.

I found new kinds of candy, which were interesting and very good. English candies were imported, and my favorite among these was Paradise Plums; they were large lozenges, red on one side, and yellow on the other. I could suck on one of those a long time. The native candies I remember most are "stuck" almonds, coconut, or "wangra" (sesame seeds, or something very similar). "Stuck" refers to the fact that sugar and water were boiled to about the consistency of fudge, and the nuts, coconut, or seeds added — thus sticking them together. (The almonds were a variety grown on the island, smaller and shaped differently from those I was familiar with. We also liked to nibble off the outer shell of the nuts when they were ripe and a bright yellow color, and had fallen from the trees.) The other native candy that I probably liked best of all was the pulp from the tamarind mixed with white sugar and then shaped into balls; it was sweet but very tart. Cayman peppermints were very nippy, snow-white, and "pulled" taffy style. I've not seen any like them anywhere else.

Coconuts were truly exotic to me — I had seen only the very dry ones in grocery stores, and not many of those. We found that Caymanian cooks used coconuts in many ways, such as coconut milk mentioned for cooking, but they also furnished on-the-spot refreshment. My parents and I visited many homes, and it was wonderful to have someone whack off the end of a green coconut with a machete and offer it to us for a delicious cool drink of the water inside. Then he would split it open, shave off a chip of the husk to use for a spoon, and we would delight in the soft jelly-like "cream" (immature meat). Nothing was more refreshing after a walk in the hot sun.

No restaurants were operating in Cayman. In the 1920s, Mrs.

Men gathered outside the market on Hog Stye Bay.

Glandore Solomon operated a rooming house in George Town providing rooms and meals for the very infrequent visitors to the island. The first meal Daddy and Mother and I ate in Cayman was breakfast at Miss Glandore's, served on Haviland china, which I had never seen before. We felt quite favored to eat at her table, and appreciated it especially because we had had no supper the night before. She introduced us to shaddock (similar to grapefruit). Local people had nowhere to eat except at home or at a friend's.

Almost all water used on the island was rain water caught and stored in cisterns, or — in the case of less-affluent families — in oil drums. The wells that existed were shallow and brackish, the water not fit for drinking.

Caymanians were quite self-sufficient in their limited diet for all but a few items such as flour, sugar, coffee, cocoa, etc. They didn't know that the starchy diet caused some problems, so they were content, and no one went hungry.

Mrs. Booker's class of 1927-28: (Front Row) Nyria Eden, Ruth Merren, Alda Parsons, Frances Booker, Aarona Booker; (Back Row) Astor Coe, Ellery Merren, Paul Bush, Byrum Bush, Silby Coe.

CHAPTER 4

Readin', 'Ritin' 'n' 'Rithmetic

S itting at my study table, I watched children and teenagers trooping along the path under the guinep tree at the back of our yard, heading for Mr. Goring's school. Mr. Goring was a lawyer who supplemented his law practice with a one-room school in his yard where he taught all ages, assisted by his oldest daughter, Edith, who taught the younger children. Teenagers studied Latin, history, composition, bookkeeping, mathematics, and text book science (he had no laboratory). His school was one of two or three private schools in George Town, another being run by Josephine and Dorothy Hutchings, daughters of the Commissioner (the highest government official, appointed by the Governor of Jamaica, as the Cayman Islands were then a Dependency of Jamaica).

Before leaving the States, I had finished the seventh grade. During the few weeks we spent in the Isle of Pines before going on to Cayman, I attended a private school that Americans living there had set up — about ten or twelve pupils, and one dubiously qualified teacher. My mother had intended to send me to the Cuban public school across the street from our dwelling, but as neither the teacher nor any of the pupils spoke a word of English, and I spoke no Spanish, she decided that would not be feasible. Furthermore, the students studied by all reading aloud at one time — quite a hubbub!

Education was compulsory and families were fined one shilling per week for each child who did not attend class. Government schools in Cayman were one-room buildings, operated under a system modeled after the English system, but going no higher than about the equivalent of sixth grade in the States. Furnishings were meager and rough, and I was intrigued by the slates that were still being used. In fact, I bought one, although I didn't actually use it for my schoolwork — it was just a novelty for me.

In both private and government schools, girls wore bright cotton

Cayman Islands

№ 164/1928

Commissioner's Office,
Grand Cayman, 17th March 192 8

Madam,

I am desired by His Honour to inform you that the
Board of Education recognises your Private School for
children of all ages.   A copy of the Regulations is
enclosed, and I am to say an Attendance Register will be
supplied if needed.

I have the honour to be,
Madam,
Your obedient servant,

C. M. Connor

Secretary Board Education.

Mrs Frances C. Booker,
Georgetown.

Approval from the Commissioner for Mrs. Booker to open a school.

dresses and shoes and stockings. Boys dressed in bright pink, green, yellow, or blue Indian Head cotton straight knee pants, long-sleeved matching jackets, and shoes and socks. Boys did not get long pants until they were fourteen or fifteen years old, and were usually out of school by then.

My parents faced a dilemma: they didn't really have the money to send me to a private school, even though the fees were modest, about one guinea (21 shillings) a quarter, and they weren't sure how well I would be prepared to enter high school at my age level when we returned home. As I had already progressed beyond the government school's highest level, that was out. They considered sending me back to live with my brother, a teacher, and his wife, but neither my parents nor I thought much of that idea. Even though I adored my brother, I did not want to be banished from Eden to Kansas!

The solution was to set up my very own private school, although neither my mother nor my father had finished high school. (They were, however, self-educated quite well, and my mother had almost finished high school.) In my bedroom was what was called a library table, and from somewhere Mother collected appropriate books. I'm not sure where she got them, but she must have had them sent from the States. I presume, since I have so little memory of what my parents did, how they did it, or how long it took, that I wasn't particularly concerned at the time about whether I went to school. I was enjoying myself immensely.

Mother set up a regular schedule for me: I was to study from nine o'clock until twelve, with a short recess and frequent consultations with Mother. She realized that an all-day schedule all by myself was not workable. At 9 A.M. I would go into my room, shut the door, settle down at my table, and get out a history book. After about fifteen minutes or so of reading history, interspersed with looking out the window, I would pull out from my stack of books something more interesting, such as *Treasure Island*. I would keep the open history book nearby, and when I heard Mother coming, I would quickly slide it over *Treasure Island*. I thought I was fooling Mother, and maybe sometimes I did, but she was smart and she knew me very well. However, she rarely made an issue of it. She knew I loved to read, and she probably thought — or at least hoped — that reading as avidly as I did, I would pick up a lot of what I needed to know.

Frequently the schedule would be interrupted, for a few hours or a few days, when we all three went to Newlands or Bodden Town or West Bay, or when Cynthia Jackson came from Savannah to visit me, or for various other reasons. I wonder now how regularly Caymanian children attended school, for I don't remember being lonely when visiting my school-age

**Commissioner Hutchings established
compulsory education and started
Grand Cayman's first public library.**

friends in those other districts. Maybe my visiting got them out of school,
too. But it was boring to study alone, so somehow my parents got together
enough money to send me to Mr. Goring's school for a month or two, so
that I could be with many of my friends. From what I remember of the school,
it was quite informal, and even almost chaotic at times, but Mr. Goring was
a very well-educated man, and he sent out many young men well prepared
to take on jobs as ship builders, bookkeepers, clerks, and so forth. Of course
the girls were not supposed to be prepared to make a living. I don't know
how much I learned, but I do remember reading about Queen Victoria in our
history book, and Caesar in Latin. I did have a wonderful time. I remember
my American penmanship didn't please Mr. Goring, for I didn't write in the
same style as Caymanians. He said I wrote more like a boy, which of course
didn't bother me at all.

Then as I reached the time when I should have been entering high school, my parents realized I had to have something more structured if I were not to be hopelessly behind when we returned home, so Mother saved up enough money from dress-making to enroll me in the Home Correspondence School in Malden, Massachusetts. When I completed a lesson and sent it in, I had to wait at least four weeks, often longer, for it to be graded and returned. That didn't seem to matter much for most subjects, but it certainly was no way to study algebra, especially as I heartily disliked algebra, and was convinced I couldn't do it! I didn't even pretend to get through more than about fifty pages of a very thick book, even with some tutoring by Smiley Connolly, who had been away to school somewhere. He was proficient in algebra himself, but he was unable to teach me anything. I had to start at the beginning when I returned to school in the States. (Interestingly, I had an excellent teacher, and discovered that I could do algebra after all!)

Eventually, on August 29, 1927, Mother opened a school in our church, which made school much more enjoyable for me. She had as many as fifteen students at one time. I know of no other church-sponsored school in Grand Cayman then, at least not in George Town. Among the pupils besides myself were Astor Coe, Ellery Merren, Ruth Merren, Paul Bush, Byrum Bush, Silby Coe, Nyria Eden, and Alda Parsons,

The only library in George Town, started by Commissioner Hutchings, was in a very small upstairs room in of the old Court House on the waterfront near Merrendale. Gentle little Miss Jane Bond Arch presided over it, but I have no idea how it was financed, or if she was paid any salary at all.

We collected some books from various places and added our own to them, and ran our own little library from our home, free to anyone who wanted to check them out. I read everything I could get my hands on, and that, with my rather casual and sketchy schooling, somehow enabled me to go into the junior class in the high school back in Mississippi with my friends and graduate with them two years later.

One of the Coe girls in Newlands, sporting the popular haircut of the day.

CHAPTER 5

Catalog Couture

O ne of the big surprises to my mother and me was how up-to-date Caymanians were in clothing styles, but we soon realized why. One reason was that men who were off the island often sent back ready-made clothing, including dresses, shoes, underwear, etc., for their families. They seemed to do a remarkable job in selecting styles and sizes. Another reason was that Montgomery Ward and Sears Roebuck Company did a lot of business on the island, and their catalogs provided styles not only through what was ordered, but as the models for clothes sewn on the island. My mother was a skilled seamstress, but she had to get used to the lack of patterns for dresses.

Men were quite conservative, wearing their white Indian Head suits whenever they were away from home (except for those doing physical labor). White pith helmets were common, as well as straw hats. Dark suits were sometimes worn for such occasions as weddings.

Some dress styles couldn't be copied in Cayman, so the girl who had one sent to her was very fortunate. The sister of my friend Alda Parsons sent her one of these dresses from Tampa — a pale pink beaded sleeveless georgette sheath. Such elegance I knew would never be mine, but when I would go down north to visit Alda, she would let me put it on, and I would parade around the house feeling like a princess.

It was a surprise to me when I discovered that I was the trendsetter for other girls, because I was the only American girl on the whole island. My mother sewed all my clothes, and soon after she made me something new, I would begin to see other girls wearing the same style. However, when I began wearing bras, I was no trendsetter — I copied mine from those the other girls had made for themselves. They were narrow, absolutely flat, cotton bands, worn as tight as we could fasten them. I suppose that was the flapper image. Our slips were also homemade of cotton, and shapeless

Author posing by the sundial on Hog Stye Bay

except for a few gathers over each hip.

I thought of myself as a tomboy, and decided to wear my hair as nearly like a boy's as my parents would allow. Rose Arch usually cut my hair, and I had her shingle it up the back (a rather new style at the time) and not very long at the sides. Then I would brush it back over my ears to make it look like a boy's. That probably caught on quicker than almost anything else, and I soon saw girls who made no pretense of being tomboys wearing their hair

Smartly dressed ladies at the launching of the Arbutus

not only like mine, but actually shingled over their ears.

Because of this tomboy bent, I was attracted to the lumberjackets that appeared — where else? — in the Sears catalog, and of course I longed for one, regardless of its unsuitability for the tropics. For my new 1926 Christmas outfit, Mother made me one out of plaid rayon with a matching pleated skirt, and I endured the long sleeves in spite of the heat. Soon the copies began to appear.

At first I wasn't sure I liked being copied, especially when they carried the style beyond what I was allowed to, but then I began to be flattered by a situation I was never to experience again.

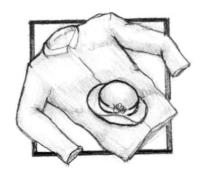

Kate Forbes and her daughter (South Church Street) using the most common mode of travel – "shanks mare".

CHAPTER 6

Sea Legs and Shanks Mare

The most electrifying sound heard on Cayman was the long-drawn-out musical cry "Sa-a-i-l ho-o-o-o!" sung out at top voice by the first person to sight a sail — a mere speck on the horizon — and taken up by everyone who heard it, and passed on in every direction. This was the first news of the arrival of a ship, and everyone "came awake" with exciting anticipation, and dropped whatever they were doing if at all possible.

All persons, goods, and mail arriving in Cayman came on native schooners, or, after about 1927, on small motor ships such as the *Cimboco*, the *Noca*, the *Nunoca*, and the *Lady Slater*. The motor ships ran more or less on a schedule (not a very reliable one), but the arrival time for any other ship was purely speculative, and sometimes totally unexpected. The ships had to anchor offshore, unloading passengers by small boat and cargo by lighters. Eventually — about 1930 — vessels arriving when the sea was calm could tie-up at the dock by Mr. Mally McTaggart's store on the north side of Hog Stye Bay.

The vessels came from various ports — Tampa, Florida, direct or by way of Nueva Gerona, Isle of Pines; Kingston or Montego Bay, Jamaica; Mobile, Alabama; Cayman Brac or Little Cayman; ports in Belize, Nicaragua, Honduras, or Costa Rica; from the Banks off Central America where they went for turtle, and occasionally from other ports.

The minimum time at sea was about one day (from Cayman Brac, for instance, in good weather), and the maximum time varied from five or six days in good weather from Tampa, to eight or ten days for a longer distance or when the weather was stormy, or when a ship without a motor was becalmed. Mother and Daddy and I were on the three-master schooner *Explicit*, powered by wind alone, when she took from noon on Friday until Monday afternoon to reach Cayman Brac — a distance of about seventy miles. We couldn't even try to estimate the actual miles covered, however, as the ship battled high seas and strong head winds all the way, constantly "tacking" — moving in a zigzag pattern — to catch the wind in the sails.

In Grand Cayman, Mr. Albert Panton was for many years the government agent for Customs and Immigration. He boarded every ship before anyone could disembark, and the process of being cleared was leisurely. Each passenger had to present identification, such as a birth certificate or a passport, unless he or she was Caymanian, in which case they would be personally known to Mr. Panton. Visitors, of whom there were very few (we saw no more than a dozen Americans in our three years there), had to show him how much money they had, to demonstrate that they could care for themselves while on the island and have enough to buy return passage (a matter of two to three pounds, equivalent to $10-$15, to Tampa, for example). And of course the ship's papers had to be inspected and the cargo cleared.

Champey Forbes delivering laundry to McCoy's Villa

While all this was proceeding slowly, people gathered on the rocks. The stores did not actually close, but they were left with few workers, and little if any business, and homes were deserted as almost everyone gathered by the sea.

Caymanians returning to the island, regardless of the time of day or night or the weather, came ashore dressed in their very best clothes. This was no small accomplishment, for travel on a little schooner did not include facilities for cleanliness, careful grooming, or privacy. I saw one woman returning from the States come ashore under the blazing sun wearing her fur coat!

My father had not noticed this custom, and so had not warned Mother and me. It was after dark when we disembarked for the first time in George Town; we were seasick, dirty, and disheveled. Therefore, we not only shocked everyone by not being dressed up, but, even more shocking, we wore knickers, apparently the first seen in Cayman. It was some time before we discovered that we had caused a great deal of criticism and comment, and I am surprised that we were accepted as warmly as we were. We didn't make that mistake again, no matter what the circumstances.

From the discovery of the islands by Columbus on May 10, 1503, until the first motor ships provided some improvement, travelling to Cayman was an adventure that required fortitude. Vessels provided no accommodations for passengers, although it was extremely rare for a ship to depart or arrive with no passengers.

This meant that the captain and mates had to vacate their cabin for the use of passengers and join the crew in the forecastle. Often male passengers also had to crowd into the forecastle, or if weather permitted, sleep on deck, which on the whole was more pleasant than the hot, stuffy, crowded forecastle, or even the cabin. My parents and I sometimes moved out on deck, with only a thin cotton blanket between us and the hard boards.

The captain's cabin was far from luxurious. On a smaller schooner such as the *Tuecoi* it might be no more than twelve feet square, equipped with bunks that would accom-modate three or four per-

Sailboats were often used to travel between Districts.

sons in all. As many more as could crowd in slept on the floor in the center. The *Tuecoi* had no sanitary facilities at all. Passengers had to bring their own washpans and buckets, to be used when a moment of privacy could be arranged. (Men used the rail.) A water tank held enough water for drinking, or for brushing one's teeth — leaning over the rail — and a little for washing one's face. As mentioned, a larger ship such as the *Antoinette* had slightly better facilities. The *Explicit* seemed downright luxurious, with two cabins in addition to the captain's cabin, a small area for eating, and a "head" (latrine).

The coming of the motorships brought in a new era, however, for they had several cabins that would hold two or more passengers, and were also equipped with "heads" (bathrooms — stool, lavatory, and a rather primitive shower, but no hot water). Such luxury had its price: passage on the *Nunoca* had gone up to seven pounds ($35.00) round trip from George Town to Tampa, including meals, by 1934.

On the schooners, food was prepared in a tiny galley, and often featured freshly-caught fish; barracuda being one of the choicest. When the

Horse-drawn cart on the dirt track between George Town and Newlands.

weather was good, meals were eaten on deck, the top of the cabin serving as the table. When the sea was too rough for on-deck dining, those who still cared to eat collected their plates of food from the galley and ate wherever they could find shelter. However, motor ships once more upgraded life at sea, having a "dining salon" furnished with tables and chairs.

In order to pass the time, passengers played cards, sang hymns or other favorites (usually someone on board had a guitar or mandolin for accompaniment), or sat talking on deck, watching the seamen fishing or sometimes spearing a shark, which provided excitement. Ships had no means of communicating with the shore or other ships, much less radio for entertainment.

Getting from place to place ashore was also primitive for many years. The most common mode of travel was by foot, "shanks mare", and almost as common was riding a bicycle, for bicycles were in great abundance. Next came riding a donkey, or, if one were more fortunate, a horse. Horse-drawn carts and buggies were another common mode of transportation. The earliest form of public transportation was probably such as that operated by Henry (Khaki) Bodden, who lived in Bodden Town. He made twice-weekly trips to George Town; his charge was six pence per passenger each way, and he crowded as many as he could into his cart. He also carried packages and letters, and took orders for provisions for those not able or desirous of making the trip. Roads were narrow and rough, either sand or marl, and an hour or two jolting in such a vehicle called for stamina. The first roads simply followed the "bush tracks" established by people on foot. Houses were built wherever people wanted them, and the paths wound around them and to them as needed. The only straight road in those days was the one from George Town to West Bay; it was straight because the strip of land it was on was too narrow for any curves, and there were no buildings or trees to go around.

My parents and I did a lot of walking, as at first we had no other means of transportation, except when we rode in a cart to Newlands or Bodden Town, or when we could get a ride in a car. My father walked to each outlying district every two or three weeks to visit and to hold services. Eventually the church bought a horse and buggy for him and Mr. Leighton Bush, a native minister, to use for church work. As the buggy would hold only two people, I rarely rode in it, but Mother sometimes rode with Daddy. When I got a bicycle for my fourteenth birthday, my father stipulated that he could also use it.

Every few weeks, we would get up very early in the morning and walk seven miles on the beach instead of the road to West Bay. We spent the day

Automobiles, such as H.O. Merren's, were rare sights on the island.

visiting church members and friends, then toward evening when it was cooler, we walked seven miles home. The beach was covered with many varieties of beautiful shells, from rice shells (almost too tiny to see), sunbeams, cowries, an occasional conch, and many others. We always took with us some kind of container, and picked up as many shells as we wanted to carry.

By about 1920, cars had begun to make their appearance on the island, but not in great numbers, as they had to be shipped from the United States on the deck of a schooner. Only the wealthier people owned cars at first, but by the time we lived there, it was not unusual for a man returning from work in the States to bring a car back with him. There were no taxis, but it was common practice to hire a car owner to take one to another district.

Anyone driving a car picked up as many pedestrians as could be packed in. Once the car was absolutely full, the driver would stop to apologize for not being able to pick up anyone else. Often he would go out of his way to deliver his passengers to their destinations.

Even after the appearance of cars, five miles was considered a long trip. People seldom visited from one settlement to another, and no one worked out of his own area. As long as we lived on the island, only a rough, rocky footpath through the bush connected North Side and East End to any other settlement, thus practically all travel to or from these districts had to be by boat. Consequently, some people of those settlements lived their entire lives without visiting another part of the island.

"I been Punishin'"

CHAPTER 7

I Been Punishin'

"All hope abandon, ye who enter here" would have been the appropriate sign to have been placed above the door of the building known as the hospital. Although there was nothing about the little unpainted shack to identify it, everyone knew it was the last resort. It stood at the beginning of Seven Mile Beach across from the present site of the Merren shopping complex, the last structure of any kind from that part of George Town until the first houses of West Bay. I don't remember that anyone was actually sent there while we were on the island, but I knew that it was where patients with a contagious disease, such as small pox or typhoid fever, could be sent. I did not know how such persons would have been cared for, but I have since been told that minimal care was supplied by an old woman who charged 1/6 (one shilling and six pence) a day, if there was no relative or friend to look after them. As my friends and I trooped by on our way to the beach, we looked at the forlorn little building with dread.

Health care was available, however, and sometimes people from other islands, such as the Isle of Pines, would come to Cayman to see the doctor. The only physician on the island while we were there was a government doctor, Dr. Overton, from Barbados, who had been educated at Howard University in Washington, D.C. His office was in his home, next to Government House, the residence of the Commissioner. He made house calls as needed, as he had one of the few cars on the island.

When Dr. Overton left the island for holidays, ailing persons consulted with Mr. Mally (Malcolm McTaggart), who owned and operated a large general store on Hog Stye Bay in George Town. He had started in medical school, but after his father's death, he dropped out in order to help his younger brother Roy finish his schooling to become a dentist. Mr. Mally acted as a pharmacist and unofficial physician, rather freely diagnosing, and dispensing simple drugs and patent medicines. In the opinion of many, he was better than some doctors, and he was considered especially effective in treating asthma.

Midwives, with little or no formal training, delivered babies. Leila Yates of West Bay received training in midwifery from Dr. Overton, and then went to Jamaica for the examination to qualify as a midwife. She delivered about one thousand babies over a period of about forty years in the homes of her patients, or in the one-room maternity "ward" she set up in her own home, to which some patients came. She had no anesthetics, no electricity, no running water, either in her own home or patients' homes, yet she says she never lost a baby or a mother. Her fee for home delivery was one pound for nine days of care, and four shillings a day if longer care was needed. In her home the fee was fourteen pounds for the entire "lying in period." Other practical nurses or midwives, also trained by Dr. Overton, were Hetty Brown, Jane Hurlston, Bella Hennings, and Annie Bush.

Obeah and folk medicine were important elements in health beliefs and practices for many years. Some men were credited with the power of obeah, although few if any, would openly proclaim this status for themselves. Spring Forbes, who lived with his common-law wife and many children on his plantation in the South Sound area, was referred to as an obeah man, but this was no doubt simply hearsay. I recall no accounts of any obeah activity on his part. Actually, obeah existed in a much milder form than in other areas of the Caribbean, having more the characteristics of folk medicine than of voodoo, and the power to affect health was often attributed to those who were not necessarily suspected of obeah. Irksie, complaining of a pain in her side, accused her neighbor Ansenitta, with whom she had quarrelled, "She put me so." Another expression indicating that someone had caused sickness was "He put his mouth on me."

With formal health care so limited, Caymanians developed a wide range of treatments and cures — folk medicine, which on the whole seemed to work quite well. When I stepped on a sea egg (sea urchin) and got its spines imbedded in my foot, I was told to pour urine over the spot; another method was to treat it with aloes. Mild stomach upsets were treated with various remedies, such as salt dissolved in water, mint tea made from either "running" mint or "Providence" mint (whatever they were), or a tea made from cerassee, which was also a tonic for the blood.

Teas were made from almost anything, it seemed: from the curiosity plant for colds, tamarind leaves to bathe measles rash, white graveyard blossoms for diabetes, breadfruit leaf or basil for high blood pressure, fever (lemon) grass for fever, white mangrove for fish poisoning, "no-yo" (spelling unknown) bush to treat sores, and "ruffled bird" plant to prevent after-birth infection or fever. Boiled wine was another after-birth treatment. The seeds of the dandelion shrub (no resemblance to dandelions found elsewhere) were parched, pounded, and made into a tea for bladder and kidney trouble. Tobacco was steeped in water which was then used to eradicate head lice, and a solution made from rosemary was considered good for the hair.

Poultices were also made from many plants. Abscesses were treated with poultices made of worry vine leaves or green pepper leaves; carbuncles were treated with a poultice of bread and brown soap. Painful joints could be eased by several kinds of poultices, such as those made from mulberry leaves, young almond leaves, or young oil nut (castor bean) leaves.

Aloes were almost a cure-all: steeped in water, the resulting solution was used as a laxative or as a shampoo! Slices of aloes were tied to the head for high blood pressure, and the sap was used to treat cuts. The pulp of aloes was also combined with cornstarch to make laxative pills.

If you had a toothache, you could choose whether to have the tooth pulled, or to try one of the folk remedies available. You could place one of various substances over the affected tooth: juniper bark scraped and made into a wad, or a tobacco leaf, or a lump of alum.

An antidote for poison was made by cracking a horse eye (sea chestnut), and eating the "meat" inside. A person suffering from asthma smoked dried rosemary for relief.

Babies' ailments or discomforts were treated with many substances. If the baby had hiccups, a piece of wet cotton was put on its forehead. A piece of asafetida on the baby's fontanelle was supposed to ward off colds. If the baby caught a cold anyway, then a piece of camphor wrapped in a cloth was placed on its chest. This next remedy seems rather gross, but I was told that rat soup was a treatment for whooping cough. I can't think of a more powerful incentive to get well!

Caymanians were very fearful of catching a cold, and very careful not to pass on a cold. Anyone with a cold would go to great lengths to avoid contact with others.

We were very fortunate to have good health and to need very few of these remedies. Dr. Overton was a friend, but the only time I can remember our family needing him professionally was when I was sick for a few days and he diagnosed yellow jaundice. The only time my father was sick, Dr. Overton was on holiday, and Daddy got advice from Mr. Mally and recovered without difficulty.

Caymanians had their own expressions for illness. Espah described her problem, "I took in with appendicitis." A headache was described as "my head is sick." Dailia was "punishin' " because her "back was sick." Urselena quit leaving her house because "I had too many fall downs." She also suffered many heart attacks: "De nex' one will carry [kill] me." Brunzie said, "I sick by my foot." "What do you?" was the inquiry to someone who was ailing.

Dental care was for many years very primitive, consisting only of the pulling of troublesome teeth if the folk remedies were ineffective. In each area of the island there was usually some man, such as Willie Bodden of West Bay, who became proficient at this and who periodically made his rounds from house to house, carrying forceps in his "bosom" (shirt front). Using no anesthetic, and without even washing the forceps between extractions (he might wipe them on a rag carried in his pocket), he would quickly yank out a tooth or teeth, and go on his way. Surprisingly, there were few cases of resulting infection. His fee: 2/6 (2 shilling and six pence) for each tooth pulled.

By the 1920s, Dr. Roy, Mr. Mally's brother, who had completed his training in the States, had set up his dental office in his home in George Town, where he carried on a wide and lucrative practice for many years. (He didn't put Willie Bodden out of work, however.) Even he was rather casual in some ways; for instance, my teeth were very crooked, and he had to pull a good tooth in order to give the others more room, and he threw it out the open window near the dental chair. (In partnership with Mr. Mally, he also became a prosperous business man.)

Because of the lack of contact between Caymanians and non-Caymanians for many years, intermarriage of blood relatives was very common, and resulted in high incidence of congenital problems for which there was no treatment on the island. Mental retardation or various forms of mental illness could not be treated locally, and the afflicted persons, referred to as "fufu" or "crazy," were cared for at home. Gyda, who was both a deaf mute and "crazy," used to wander about George Town, gesturing wildly and babbling. Children were afraid of her, but she was harmless. However, she was not homeless; and she was cared for by relatives. The proportion of people who were deaf mutes was much higher than in other societies, and no professional help or schooling was available. Many of them were highly intelligent, and worked out their own systems of sign language. Children with cleft palates, of which there were many, had to be sent away for surgery. However, for lack of money, many had to live out their lives without correction.

In spite of poor nutrition and lack of up-to-date medical facilities and treatment, the Caymanians were for the most part sturdy, hard-working people, with little time nor inclination for hypochondria.

When all remedies and treatment failed, or when a death occurred on any of the Cayman Islands, the funeral followed very quickly. There was no waiting for relatives to arrive, for any who were off the island could not have returned to Cayman in less than several weeks even if the news could have reached them.

Coffins were made by local carpenters, who kept boards of varying lengths on hand, ready to be nailed together and given a coat of quick-drying varnish when a death occurred. It was the usual practice to clothe the body in a white shroud, which could be quickly run up by a local seamstress. If a death was anticipated, both the coffin and the shroud were prepared ahead

Burials took place in family plots or churchyard cemeteries.

of time. In fact, some people, recognizing the inevitability of death, preferred to take care of the details themselves. A coffin would be ordered and then stored until needed, sometimes for years. As Caymanian houses had very little if any storage space, the most convenient and out-of-the-way place to keep a coffin was under the bed. If a woman wanted something more elaborate than the hastily-made shroud, she would have a dress stored away in a box.

Burial followed death within twenty-four hours at the most. There was no means of preserving a body either by refrigeration or by embalming, so haste was necessary. Burial commonly took place on the day of the death, unless it occurred too late in the day. Of course, if a death occurred on board ship more than a certain twenty-four hours from port, burial was at sea.

Digging a grave was hard work, for rock lay close to the sandy surface in many places. However, digging a grave in sand was just as difficult, as the sand slid back into the grave as soon as it was shovelled out. Of course the digging was done without any more sophisticated equipment than a pick and shovel.

After the body was lowered into the grave, the family of the deceased and anyone else who cared to threw handfuls of sand on the coffin. Everyone stayed at the site until the grave was filled and smoothed over, then the grave was decorated with fresh hibiscus blossoms or orchids or other flowers which had been gathered from yards or the bush.

Family graveyards near the homes were used more than public cemeteries for many years. Each family maintained its own plot, usually in or adjoining the yard.

Wherever graves were located, they were meticulously cared for. Some were surrounded by a narrow white lime strip, the resulting "box" filled with sand; some were covered by a white lime slab, but most were simply mounded with sand, which was carefully swept and spread with new sand several times a year. Croton bushes were often planted around the graves, but locally-called jasmine trees (really frangipani) were so popular for

George Town Cemetary: graves of peaked beach sand lined with conch shells and headed by "graveyard trees" (frangipani)

graveyards that they were called graveyard trees.

Found in a few places, such as around the Presbyterian Church on the waterfront in George Town and near the sea at Prospect, were graves dating back to the 1700s, which were characterized by the white lime daub covered rock structure that resembled a small peaked house. Names and other information that had been placed on a small recessed mahogany square at the front had been rendered nearly illegible by the ravages of time and weather.

Funerals were very well attended, and several ministers of different faiths would conduct the service. There was no hearse on the island, so a wagon was used to take the body to the cemetery, or pallbearers carried it if the distance was short.

Mourning was observed very strictly by many people, especially by the women and the wealthier class. Black was worn for one year. After that, the women could wear white, or black and white clothes, for a year before returning to pastels. Men wore a black arm band for at least twelve months. The women of large, extended families often could not get out of some form of mourning for years, because by the time pastels were appropriate, for instance, another member of the family would have died, and they were back to black again. Aunt May Jackson, our neighbor, had simply given up — she wore nothing but black.

Pictures of the deceased in the coffin were often taken and displayed in the home. Part of the reason for this may have been that, as families off the island could not return for the funeral, this practice gave them the opportunity for a last view, thus sharing in the experience in a way. As there was no good photographer on the island, and few people had cameras — and these only simple box cameras — these pictures were at best of very poor quality and very depressing, but highly cherished nevertheless.

*Visiting author, George Allan England, inspecting finished
coils of thatch rope*

CHAPTER 8

Making a Living

F inancial affairs on the island were very simple, and debt seemed to be almost non-existent. Caymanians paid cash, and waited for what they could not pay for. I remember no banks, but I did hear that there was a Government Savings Bank operating out of Government House. Money sent from abroad came as bank drafts or checks, which were accepted at shops at an exchange rate that remained constant as long as we were there: one pound (20s) equalled US $4.80. At first I was at a complete loss trying to understand the English money and the names for the different coins and bills, but before long I could rattle off "shilling" "six pence" "threepence" and "farthing" and figure out totals and change at the shops. Eventually I even learned to multiply and divide using the three columns for pounds, shillings, and pence, but that wasn't easy. I still have an English sixpence that I saved because it was so old — it is dated 1834, and is in excellent condition.

Opportunities for making a living on the island were very limited, much more so for women than for men. The only industries, if they could be called that, were shipbuilding and rope making. Most men went to sea, a limited number on Caymanian schooners, engaged in trade or turtling, but most on merchant marine ships of other nations. The growing of "ground provisions" and butchering gave income for some persons, and shop-keepers employed a few people, chiefly men. A few men in each district made their living as carpenters.

Government jobs — post office, roads and building repair, teaching, clerical, etc. — gave employment to a few people, but government operations were uncomplicated, not time-consuming. The government doctor was not Caymanian, and there was no hospital nor dental clinic. A few people, mostly men, were employed in shops, and some men and women scrabbled out an existence on their little "plantations," digging

Some people found work with Government in the Court House Building.

among the rocks with a machete, growing ground provisions of yams, cocos, sweet potatoes, pumpkins, bananas, and so forth. Prices were low: a bunch of bananas sold for one shilling. Some of these "farmers" had cows, and sold a little milk at times. Some people combined two or more part-time occupations, such as fishing, grave-digging, pulling teeth, barbering, and making and exporting thatch rope.

A woman had very few ways to make a living available to her. She could be a seamstress if she could develop the necessary skills and obtain a sewing machine. Failing this, she could work as a maid in a home, but class entered into this alternative. Women of the higher social class would not lower themselves to such employment, even if they were penniless. Observing this, I told my mother that it seemed women either had servants, or were servants. A few women, such as the Merren daughters, for instance, worked in family-owned shops.

Many women wove baskets from tops (thatch palm fronds). Most of the baskets were made for their own home use, but some were sold to those who did not wish to make their own. Everyday hats for men, women, and children were also hand-woven from tops. For more dressy wear, beautiful hats for women were crocheted from sisal fiber as fine as sewing thread. Doilies were also crocheted from sisal. A little money might be earned from these activities.

I developed a few enterprises to make money. I ordered greeting cards in black and white from the States, tinted them with water colors, and sold them to friends. The only greeting cards sold in the shops were from England — the front covers were embossed celluloid, such as I had never seen before. Also, I tinted pictures my father printed for those who wanted that service. I also became quite good at making roses from crepe paper, dipped in melted paraffin, and I sold a few of those. My parents added to their barely adequate income — my father developed and printed pictures, and Mother sewed.

Beauty shops were unheard of, but as bobbed hair had been accepted for girls (adult women still wore their hair long), some women learned to cut hair by practicing on family members and picked up a little money by giving haircuts for about one shilling. Rose Arch was very good at this, and I got most of my haircuts from her.

There were barbers, but no barbershops, except that of the photographer in George Town who also cut hair in his shop. Every district had several men who cut hair. The barber would do business either at the patron's home or his own home, and clean-up was made very simple by working either on a porch or in the yard under a tree. They, too, charged one shilling a haircut.

For most women and children, the making and exporting of thatch palm rope provided a little income, but making rope was very hard work, and brought in very little money. The women had to first cut the thatch, sometimes going as much as three or four miles for it, carry it home, cure it, and then twist it. The rope was manufactured outdoors, often along the beach, in the "rope walk." The "pegs" (strips of unopened tops of the thatch palm, sun-dried) were threaded into the triple-grooved "cob", then the triple-cranked "cart" was turned in one direction, while the "winch", about a hundred yards away, was turned in the other direction. The rope then had to be coiled, and carried on their backs to the shops or to the boats to be shipped away. It took about a day to gather enough tops for six coils of rope, and at most, only three coils could be turned out in a day. Rope sold for about one shilling for twenty-five fathoms (one coil). As it took two or three people to produce this much, the total income for a day was little if any more than sixpence for each.

Turtling, for many years a most profitable industry, was still flourishing, but the ships were having to go farther for their catch, as turtles were rarely seen in Cayman waters any more. Except for turtles brought home for butchering, turtlers depended on American outlets, except for a small amount sold in Jamaica and other foreign ports. Both the meat and the shell were sold.

Prohibition was in force in the United States while we were in Cayman, and many Caymanians were engaged in bootlegging, one of the most lucrative occupations for seamen at that time. The only other American living in Cayman when we did was a captain who was an exile because he was wanted in the States on bootlegging charges. He made the best of the situation, settling permanently in Cayman and marrying a Caymanian woman. He seemed to be quite well off and lived in comfort. Many Caymanian seamen were not so fortunate. They were caught before amassing anything resembling a fortune, and were either jailed or deported, never again able to work on American ships or even go into American ports.

This industry is obliquely referred to in Colonial Reports by mention under "Imports and Exports." According to the Report of 1923, more than half the total of imports "represented the value of liquors imported from Cuba and re-shipped to that island and the Bahamas." Apparently the government did not wish to acknowledge the true destination — the United States — nor the law-breaking nature of the industry.

Shipbuilding was the main industry of the island, Cayman-built schooners being much in demand for many years. The builders had no

Too rocky to plough or spade, "plantations" were often worked with a machete.

Ship building was the island's main industry.

engineering education; they worked with painstaking, loving care without plans, blue-prints, specifications or machinery. The only guides used by the builders were a whittled-out model and a rough sketch of the sails on a board. Every timber was worked out with adz and saw from mahogany, fiddlewood, pompero, or ironwood, grown right on the island. Only the planking, sticks (masts), canvas, and engines (if any) were imported. The sails were cut out on the beach. Eight or ten men could build a seventy-foot schooner in about nine or ten months. Four or five ships were usually under construction on the island at any one time. The builders I especially remember were James Arch and his sons, who built about forty vessels, and Captain Rayal Bodden, who built about the same number, including the first motor ships, the *Cimboco* and the *Lady Slater*.

Most men eventually came home to stay, when they were too old or too sick to work. Sometimes a man would return after years of absence with no communication with his family, which meant that the family had had a very hard time getting along. Some men saved enough money to establish themselves on the island in some little business. Some took their families off the island to live, but many of these returned to Cayman for retirement. (Many men, of course, were lost at sea, or died away from home.)

It was not an easy life, but Caymanians — men, women, and children — managed to accept life and its problems and hardships with equanimity and serenity.

*Bob Fink (left), an American artist, chatting with an
unidentified Caymanian outside of Mally McTaggart's shop.*

CHAPTER 9

Heard on the Marl Road

E na Jackson requests the honour of your presence at a party at her home Friday evening, February 6." So read the formal heading at the top of a most informal sheet of lined paper, followed by a list of names of those being invited. No address was needed, as everyone knew where everyone else lived. Indeed, no one actually had an address, other than the name of the settlement. A small black boy was usually the courier, carrying the invitation from house to house, with each person checking his or her name, and indicating acceptance or regrets.

The only telephones on the island were very primitive, with only one in each of the settlements of Bodden Town, George Town, and West Bay, used only by government officials for government business, or for emergencies. Thus private communication had to take place face to face, by the method just described, or by letter. Tri-weekly mail services, between settlements, carrying mostly official mail, were maintained by the constables. Most local and private letters, and even many going abroad, however, were not posted, but carried by hand by someone who would be seeing the addressee — "Avanza Rivers, by Lecensy Barnes," for instance. People seldom asked for mail at the post office except when a boat had come in.

The only communication with Cuba or the Isle of Pines, Jamaica, the coasts of Central America, or the southern ports of the United States was by trading schooners. Communication between Grand Cayman and the two lesser islands was possible only through the sporadic visits of the small schooners. According to the Colonial Reports for the era, "There is little of community interest between Grand Cayman and the smaller islands, and inter-communication is irregular." Cayman Brac and Little Cayman were apparently left much on their own, with little interest or interference from the authorities in George Town, and only an annual visit by the Commissioner.

When a ship arrived with mail, the mail bags would be brought ashore in the government launch, and people eager for mail would soon fill the lobby of the small post office on Hog Stye Bay in George Town to overflowing. Those who couldn't crowd inside stood out in the hot sun. As the clerk removed each piece from the bag, he would call out the name: Ephenetus Forbes, Enginnia Bodden, Alric Watler, and on and on. This made for a very long and tedious process if there was a lot of mail; it would take a half day or more. The longest we ever went without mail while we lived there was six weeks, and then the mail bags were very full indeed. If, after a number of calls, a piece of mail was not claimed, it was laid aside to be claimed later, and the next name called.

My father would go to the post office and claim mail until he had a large bundle, which he would bring home to Mother and me. Back he would go, and repeat the process until he had all our mail. Meantime, Mother and I

Young ladies out for a stroll, catching up on the latest "marl road" news?

eagerly opened letters and shared news. We usually spent two or three days reading and rereading letters.

No newspaper was published on the island, and none from abroad were shipped in for sale. In March, 1926, my mother wrote to friends in Florida, asking them to please send a newspaper, as we had not seen one since leaving Florida the previous October. Daddy, who was an avid baseball fan, later arranged for relatives in Mobile, Alabama, to save copies of the *Mobile Register* for him during the baseball season and send them down when the *Explicit* came every six weeks or so. He then read them in order, savoring the baseball news over several days. If the climax of the season came just after the *Explicit* had left Mobile, he had to wait in suspense for several more weeks to find out if his favorite club, the Washington Senators, were world champs.

Because of no radio, wireless, or newspapers, news from abroad literally trickled in, surprisingly often by the popular phonograph records sent home that were about tragic or very newsworthy events. "The Death of Floyd Collins" centered on a man trapped in a cave; "The Wreck of the Shenandoah" told of the crash of a dirigible. A group of my friends and I were walking to Smith's Barcadere to go in the sea when someone began singing a song about "Lucky Lindy, flew all alone." None of us had the slightest idea who Lucky Lindy was, nor where nor why he flew alone, but we loved the song, and sang lustily. It was several weeks before we heard

"*Shooting the Breeze,*" on the seawall on Hog Stye Bay

about Charles Lindberg's solo flight across the Atlantic — the greatest news story of the time.

Local news travelled amazingly fast: it was "heard on the marl road," and within a few hours people from West Bay to Bodden Town would know that Aunt Sevonia Jackson had died that morning and the funeral would be at 3 P.M., or that Trenvic and Nassaria Hydes had a baby girl.

The fastest travelling news item was that of the arrival of a ship. Within about fifteen or twenty minutes of the first sound of "Sail ho" the news had reached from West Bay to Bodden Town. It was uncanny that by this time everyone who could see the ship knew "Dat be de Bluefish out of Belize. She lef' Tuesday mornin'. Granston Ebanks be on her, too, and she laden wit' turtle." Most of the time all the information was correct down to the details. This was truly remarkable considering that no ships ran on a regular schedule, and there was no ship-to-shore nor ship-to-ship communication, nor any cable or wireless between Cayman and the rest of the world.

The only warning Caymanians had of an approaching hurricane was from watching the barometer and the action of the sea and the clouds. Those who were knowledgeable did a good job of predicting, but it was at best imprecise, and it took some time for news of a hurricane's path and destruction to reach the island. I remember the day that the *Lady Antoinette* slowly made her way past McCoy's Villa, badly damaged, with both her masts gone, after being battered by the edge of a hurricane. Everyone had been anxiously waiting for her appearance, or for news of her, but this was the first anyone knew of what had happened to her.

After a bad storm, communication of news on the island was difficult, for it didn't take a very strong gale to blow down the flimsy telephone lines, and heavy seas would wash rocks and other debris over the roads so that travel between settlements was slowed down or stopped. My mother and I were caught in Bodden

Walking down the marl road on Hog Stye Bay.

Town when the hurricane of October 18, 19, and 20, 1926, hit. My father was several miles away in Savannah, with no way of finding out whether we had got home to George Town. Fearing for our safety, he walked about seven miles along the Prospect-Red Bay road, up to his waist in surging sea water covering the road, only to find we were not at home. For two days he could get no word from Bodden Town. On Thursday, when the hurricane had passed, Mother and I had no way to get home except to walk, as the roads were blocked to cars or carts with rocks and other debris, and we had no horse to ride. We walked about twelve miles, around and through puddles and around large and small boulders and tree limbs and coconut fronds. My mother, as we came to each place where the road was covered with water, would take off her shoes to wade through, then put them on again. At the first big puddle, I took off my shoes and carried them several miles until we reached our home. I was used to going barefoot. It was ten days before the roads were at all passable for cars or wagons.

It was two weeks after the storm before we received any news from the rest of the world. We then learned that the Isle of Pines had been almost wiped out. Sixty-five percent of the buildings had been destroyed, and all the rest damaged. Many lives were lost, including William Davis, his wife, and three of their five children, Caymanians who were members of our church.

With such infrequent and sketchy news from abroad, we lived our lives with little concern for what was happening in the rest of the world.

Churches, such as the RLDS shown here, were a major source of social activity.

CHAPTER 10

Merrymaking Island Style

A phonograph — and records! I was delighted to find these among the furnishings of McCoy's Villa when we moved in. We had never had a phonograph before, so this was real luxury, although I didn't really feel a great need for a way to entertain myself. With no commercial entertainment, we still had lots of fun, for Caymanians made their own good times. Swimming — "going in the sea," as Caymanians put it — was very popular, as was bicycle riding in pairs or especially in groups. Parties and dances were given frequently, and any concert — all purely amateur — drew crowds of people. Both younger and older people enjoyed walking together; not walking for exercise, but just strolling along and talking or singing. Ship launchings, which were really hard work, became social events, and church activities, including funerals, also served a social function.

Parties were enjoyed by children, youth, and adults, most being held in homes. Occasionally, however, a party would be large enough to require the use of the Town Hall. This was often true of the very popular costume parties. All costumes had to be made on the island, and they were quite imaginative and elaborate. The person would decide what personage he or she wanted to be, such as Cleopatra or Uncle Sam, and then go to a dressmaker to have the costume made. My mother made many of these, and I helped with the trimming after the basic sewing was done. I remember making about fifty pink rosebuds from crepe paper for one dress.

Caymanian seamstresses not only made clothes for women and children, but also the white suits most men wore for dress, all these without commercial patterns. Eddie Parsons, for instance, would take one of his suits and the material to the seamstress, who would then in a few days have his new suit ready for him. She would also sew for his wife, Mary-Annie, who would provide a dress that fit her, her material, and a picture of what she wanted, usually from a catalog. That was all the seamstress needed. It was no problem, then, for the seamstress to produce a costume for the Queen of Sheba, Uncle Sam, or Little Boy Blue, provided she had a garment and a good description or picture to go by. At the party prizes were awarded for the best costumes, sometimes in several categories.

Caymanians were lovers of music. They loved to sing, and almost every home had some kind of musical instrument, such as organ, piano, guitar, mandolin, fiddle, or sometimes two or three of these. Many homes had phonographs, and I remember when Capt. Ben Lyons brought in the first orthophonic record player, the latest thing out. Everyone enjoyed dancing to the music provided by a phonograph. Caymanians were remarkably up-to-date on music, as those working in the States sent home the most popular records as soon as they were produced. Returning seamen always brought some of the latest home with them too.

Whoever was hosting the party provided refreshments of sandwiches, cakes, and lime- or lemonade, or drinks made from fruit syrups. Occasionally some liquor might be served, but excessive drinking or drunkenness seldom occurred at these parties. I got my information about the dances from my friends who could attend, or from looking in from the outside, as our church members frowned on dancing. (My parents never discussed the issue specifically, but I realized that they didn't consider dancing itself sinful, for they said nothing when my friend Alda and I cranked up the phonograph and danced in our living room.)

People who were not included in "society" functions held dances with music provided by local musicians, playing fiddles or guitars, graters, and home-made drums. The graters were just that — holes punched with big nails in heavy tin, played by rubbing a fork or other metal object up and down in rhythm. Liquor was more common at these functions, which were usually held outside, and as the evening wore on, drunken brawls often broke out, which gave the constables a little real police work.

When Pentecostal missionaries came to the island, their converts shunned most of the social functions, particularly those that included dancing and/or drinking, or even the singing of popular songs. Singing "The Pagan Love Song" was definitely considered sinful, for instance.

Concerts were also popular entertainment. They were held all during the winter months, but especially during the Christmas season. A concert consisted not only of musical numbers (sometimes none), but also of readings, plays, and pageants. Some were given by private schools, but many were produced by anybody who just wanted to do so and who could get volunteers to perform, and it wasn't hard to do that. Most were held at

***Ruth Merren, Hebe Bodden, Ena Merren, and Dorothy
Hutchings relaxing on the beach after a swim***

Eddie Parsons dressed as Uncle Sam

the Town Hall. Admission was usually six pence for general admission, and 1 or 2 shillings for reserved seats, the resulting revenue going to some worthy cause.

As there was no other form of public entertainment, attendance at concerts was always good, even though everyone knew the quality of some performances would be hilariously poor, such as anything produced by Martha Saunders. She created her own material, which included such characters as the Queen of the Fairies, witches, and elves, with no discernible plot. I was once conscripted to be Queen of the Fairies in one of her concerts. All of us in the cast made fun of her behind her back, I'm ashamed to say, and were relieved when the evening was over—but we didn't refuse to take part! Martha's eccentricities were quite apparent in her appearance. She refused to have her picture taken, so my father snapped one of me while she was adjusting my costume, and thus managed to get her picture, too.

Moonlight picnics were favorite activities of teen-agers. A group would form and walk to a beach, each one taking some food along. In the outlying districts, such as Savannah, a few boys would ride horses to the beach, usually having a race along the way. When everyone reached the beach, they would sit on the sand and sing, and some would go in the sea. Very seldom did couples pair off and drift off to themselves. Their romantic inclinations were satisfied by the playing of ring games. I can almost feel the breeze on my skin, and see the bright moonlight streaming across the water, as we circled around, holding hands, and singing "Go in and out the window" or "Rice, peas, beans and barley grow." The boy or girl who was It chose a partner, ran around the circle, received a kiss, and the chosen one then became It, and so on. It is hard for me to believe that we went on these picnics unchaperoned, but I don't remember the chaperones if there were any, so they must not have interfered with our fun to any extent. The picnics would break up and everyone would go home by about 10 o'clock.

One moonlight picnic at Savannah stands out in memory, not because of the picnic itself, of which I remember practically nothing, but because of the horse race I became involved in. We were staying for a few days at Lina and Farrell Jackson's home in Newlands. They owned Diablo, a beautiful black horse that was renowned for his speed, although he was a little past his prime by then. Horse races were simply informal, spontaneous affairs along the road. I was allowed to ride Diablo that night to the picnic, and there were three or four others on horseback. When we started home, I was trotting along comfortably, when Halley Coe, who was a deaf-mute, rode up beside me, and by sign-language indicated that he wanted to race. I wasn't a particularly skilled rider, and I had no desire to race, but there was no point in yelling "No" when he couldn't hear me, and I couldn't spare a hand to signal a refusal even if I had known how, so matters were taken out of my hands when Halley started off. It so happened that Diablo would not allow another horse to get ahead of him if he could help it, and without any decision on my part, we took off at a gallop. I had nothing to do with the race except to hang on while Diablo pounded along, with me jouncing up and down in the saddle, hanging on to the pommel.

The race didn't last long, for in less than a mile Diablo had saved his pride, and I had saved mine by managing not to fall off. The consequence was that Halley told everyone (by signs) about the race and about what a good rider I was. I basked in my little bit of fame, not once admitting that all the credit should have gone to Diablo.

We also frequently went to the beach for picnics in the afternoon, but there was more swimming then, more horseplay. We had to go off among the sea grape trees to put on our swim suits, and to dress after swimming without any way of rinsing off the salt water.

Children had great fun bicycling, going in the sea, spinning tops, sailing home-made model sailboats, or playing rounders (a British forerunner of baseball). My father introduced baseball, modified to fit the confines of our yard, for kids who came to play with me. Tennis was popular in George Town for teenagers and young adults. Just south of Dr. Roy McTaggart's home were two courts, surfaced with marl, which were much used by the "upper crust" of the town. Our family introduced crokinole and carroms (board games) to the island, and hardly a week went by without one or two evenings being spent playing with groups of friends who stopped in.

The mosquito season, the four months of summer, drastically affected evening activities. Almost all after-dark events had to be cancelled until the mosquitoes were gone, as it was most unpleasant to be out of doors. Churches, the Town Hall, and many homes did not have screened windows, so even indoor activities were of necessity limited. Nevertheless, a few evening gatherings were held inside, with smoke pots at the door to ward off the mosquitoes. However, we confined most of our social activities to daytime fun, until the mosquitoes abated.

Author dressed as Queen of the Fairies for a concert produced by Martha Saunders

Church services provided other opportunities for people to get together, and church attendance was good, particularly at evening services. My diary contains many references to going to church for preaching, prayer service, or class, sometimes on several consecutive nights. We also occasionally had meetings at 5 P.M. Everyone dressed in their best, and women and girls almost always wore hats. In fact, it was mandatory to wear hats at the Presbyterian Church, but our church was a little more liberal about that, especially for younger girls. Women also had to wear hats for any public function, such as attendance at court, and in fact wore hats most of the time when out of doors. Men always wore suits to church and to other public functions, and also wore hats when outside. The tropical pith helmet was frequently seen.

Almost everyone walked to church, sometimes for miles. Some of our church members walked from Spotts or Red Bay, six or seven miles each way, for both morning and evening services on Sunday and to evening services during the week even after a day of hard work.

The predominant church in Grand Cayman was the Presbyterian Church of Scotland, with a minister sent from Scotland to supervise the congregations in the different districts as well as in George Town. The Baptist Church was the largest denomination in Cayman Brac, but it had no congregation in Grand Cayman. The Seventh Day Adventists had some members in Grand Cayman, with a minister from abroad sometimes on the island, but no church building. The Reorganized Church of Jesus Christ of Latter Day Saints (of which my father was a minister) was brought to Grand Cayman in 1921. It had a church building in George Town, and three missions meeting in other districts while we were there. In 1926 the Pilgrim Holiness Church was established in two or three districts, and grew quite rapidly.

Outlying districts were visited by the supervising ministers who lived in George Town, West Bay, or Bodden Town. For instance, Reverend Dixon, a Scottish minister for the Presbyterian Church, who lived with his wife and son in George Town, visited North Side once every quarter, having to make the trip by boat from George Town Barcadere across North Sound. Between visits of these ministers, local workers carried on the church work with great zeal. The social function of the churches was as important as the religious aspect, and we spent many hours at church.

Although I remember occasionally being a little homesick for the States, I don't remember ever being bored and unable to find something to do.

Police Station and Jail on Elgin Avenue where "Pegleg" was incarcerated

CHAPTER 11

Unlocked Doors

C rime was no problem on Grand Cayman. In fact, we never locked a door, although I suppose there must have been locks on the doors of McCoy's Villa before we moved in. I don't think anyone locked their house doors, however, I suppose government offices and businesses must have been locked at night.

Not many years before we arrived on Grand Cayman, a young girl's body had been found in the bush in the Newlands area, but the murder was never solved. That was the only murder I ever heard about. Fights sometimes erupted between drunken men, but these were not frequent, and were easily broken up. The constables were rarely busy, but they looked impressive in their navy blue trousers with a red stripe down each leg, their white jackets, and white billed caps or pith sun helmets.

One incorrigible thief was known as Pegleg. He had lost one leg below the knee when he was a very young man, and walked with the aid of a home-made wooden "peg leg." Occasionally he would take on a small job, but for the most part he existed by petty theft and the charity of others.

Several times he had been caught stealing and had been put in the seldom-used jail yard attached to the little police station in George Town. And several times he had escaped, only to be shortly recaptured, of course, for on such a small island there was no place to hide for long.

The jail yard was no more than a roofless pen, fifteen or twenty feet square, enclosed by a concrete wall, about seven or eight feet high, topped with broken bottles (their sharp edges long ago dulled) embedded around the top. In one corner was a simple tin-roofed shelter.

One day Pegleg was caught stealing some clothes off a line, and was taken to jail. But having learned from sad experience that it was hard to keep him in custody, and not wanting to go to the trouble of finding him again,

The local constable standing in the gateway of the Booker home on Shedden Road

the police took away his peg leg, leaving him only a short, rough, forked tree limb to use as a crutch.

On the third morning of his incarceration, when Constable Nixon arrived at the jail to check on Pegleg and give him his breakfast of bread, coffee, and avocado, Pegleg was gone! The news spread quickly along the marl roads and the waterfront.

Men slapped their knees and chuckled at his cunning. "But you no hear what Pegleg done? Dey can't keep 'im in no jail yard, no, mon." Nasaria reported some cassava missing; Ventrimena proclaimed that two loaves of fresh-baked bread were gone from her caboose; stewed turtle was gone from Neoma's kitchen; plantains and bananas from Jimima's "cookrum", and Bunyan's fishing line was missing. Soon people were vying for the distinction of having been "t'iefed" of "prowisions" by Pegleg, and the stories seemed to grow with each telling. Whymon seemed almost proud of the fact that Pegleg had stolen his catboat, and apparently put to sea in it, with his ample store of pilfered provisions.

Soon the experts announced their conclusions that Pegleg had hoisted the small sail, and without compass or chart, had set sail for Central America. Some thought he was heading for Honduras, some Nicaragua, some Belize. They examined the sky, tested the wind, read the barometer, and predicted, with admiration and confidence, "Yas, mon, he make it! He make Honduras or Nicaragua in few days' time true — unna see if he don't."

Pegleg must have felt that he could not disappoint his admirers, for true, in a few weeks his mother received a scrawled note from Pegleg in

Honduras. However, he did not reveal details of how he had scaled the wall, made his way about without his peg leg, collected provisions for the journey, stolen and launched a catboat, and reached the Central American coast without navigational instruments.

Actually, such a feat was not particularly difficult for a man of Cayman. Caymanian seamen had made their way anywhere they wished to sail, long before they had any navigational aids more sophisticated than those they devised themselves, using a stick with one notch for the horizon and another for the North Star to give them the latitude.

Traffic accidents were non-existent, as the roads were too crooked and narrow to permit any speeding on the part of the few cars. The road to West Bay was straight, but just one track, and sandy. I got a big thrill out of taking a ride once in awhile on that road with Arthur Bodden after he came home from Florida with a car. He let me steer — from the passenger side of the seat — and with no other vehicles in sight, he actually speeded up to forty miles an hour — for about a mile!

With no crime more serious than petty offenses, no one lived in fear of his life or his property. My parents let me roam as I wished quite freely, so long as I observed the "home by dark" rule.

Crime was of so little concern that it was not even mentioned in the Colonial Reports until 1927. The entry for "Justice, Police, and Prisons" begins; "There is no serious crime." The Police Force for all three islands consisted of an Inspector and six constables, the duties of the latter being largely the transfer and delivery of mails.

Exploring the Island's flora and fauna: Ruth Merren, Aarona Booker, Alda Parsons, and Frances Booker.

CHAPTER 12

There Be Dragons

S ummer months brought mosquitoes in such hordes that I can hardly believe now that they were so bad. In the heat of the day they retired for a long siesta, but with the coming of darkness they swarmed out by the millions. A dark cloud of mosquitoes followed any person out walking between dusk and daylight, and a smoke pot was a necessary item. This was a can wired with a bale, or a small bucket, filled with smoldering buttonwood that gave off thick smoke. This "pot" was carried in one's hand and swung about one's body. If guests were expected at a home, a smoke pot was placed outside the door. The visitors then paused in the smoke before slipping quickly through the door. The other defense was mosquito brushes, made of sisal, about a foot long; you really needed two, one in each hand (if you weren't carrying a smoke pot), which you could swing rhythmically, one around your head and shoulders while the other swished around your legs. As you swung the brushes, you could actually feel the mosquitoes sliding across your arms.

I learned something about killing mosquitoes that pounced on me for a meal. I was familiar with the swat method, which often missed, of course. When the first mosquito season arrived a few months after we did, I watched in amazement as Consie, seeing a mosquito on her arm, casually and slowly placed her finger on it, mashed it, and threw it to the floor. The mosquito had never realized he was in danger. Try it — it works!

To avoid the danger of being suffocated by mosquitoes clogging their nostrils, cows and horses had to be protected by smoke pots, or by logs set afire to smolder through the night. Unwary humans also faced this danger. I heard of one man so foolish as to start home late one night after he had been drinking heavily. He passed out by the side of the road, and by the time someone came along and found him, he was not only covered by bites, but had almost been smothered. He was rescued just in time.

Another predator of humans and animals was the tick, especially in rural areas such as Newlands. Dipping vats for cows were set up in four locations about the island. I thought it was great fun to get on a horse and help Marvick Smith drive Farrell Jackson's cows from Newlands to Savannah to the vat, and force them, bawling and scrambling, down the chute into the vat of something that smelled like tar. The installation of dipping vats eventually succeeded in reducing the tick pest somewhat.

Snakes were not native to the island, probably having arrived hidden in provisions such as bunches of bananas or plantains, and were not poisonous, never known to harm anyone. Occasionally one might get into a house, causing quite a commotion. One night when my friends and I were playing hide-and-seek in the Merrens' yard, one crawled across my leg as I hid under a croton bush, but I wasn't frightened enough to reveal my hiding place.

Rats and mice had also been involuntarily imported, but were only a minor nuisance. Only once did a rat get in our house, and my father succeeded in killing it with a stick.

Other creatures fascinated me. I liked the tiny little green tree frogs, and had fun putting one on the end of my finger and chasing my friend Victoria, who would run away, screaming in fright. I liked to look for "gold bugs" — a beetle, I suppose, slightly larger than a ladybug, that shone in the sun like 18 carat gold.

I heard frequent references to rabbits. One day I saw some small brown short-haired creatures with little ears in a cage in a backyard, and I asked what they were. "Why, rabbits, of course," was the answer. They didn't look the least like any rabbit I had ever seen. I eventually learned that they were agoutis.

Parrots were plentiful, as were the little yellow birds and many others I didn't recognize. The parrots were smaller than those I had seen elsewhere, and had short tails, but they could be tamed and taught to talk. One day my parents and I were walking along a road in Savannah when we spied a parrot on a porch. "Hello, Polly; hello, Polly," my Dad kept calling to it as we continued to walk along. The parrot tilted his head to one side and watched us, making no sound. Just as we got a little past the house, we heard him call out, "Who dat was, Mama?"

Summer months brought out the huge land crabs, which in settlements lived mostly in the rock walls that lined many of the roads, or in uninhabited areas in rocks and coral. They usually stayed hidden in the daytime usually, but swarmed out at night, rustling loudly through dry leaves, and covering roads with their crushed bodies, smashed by cars or wagons.

When we went in the sea, we had to watch out for the beautiful Portuguese man-of-war; if one touched your skin, it caused pain, red blotches, and extreme itching. Sea eggs were also to be avoided; they are the porcupines of the sea. If one is stepped on, it imbeds its long black quills in the flesh, causing intense stinging pain.

A land-based hazard was the maiden plum shrub. If a twig or limb was broken, sap oozed out; if this touched the skin, and was not washed away immediately, an ugly sore soon formed wherever the sap had touched, and it was difficult to heal. I suffered this kind of injury only once.

The worst infection I got in Cayman was when I skinned my leg on coral in the sea at Bodden Town, and did not clean the abrasion with alcohol as soon as I came out of the water. In a day's time, I had a large festering sore, oozing pus, which took two or three weeks to heal.

No dangerous wild creatures have ever existed in Cayman's history, either on land or in the sea. Even the dreaded sharks, barracudas, and sting rays seemed, in Cayman waters, to be quite harmless, if unmolested. Iguanas lived in the interior of the island, but were seldom seen, and although they looked like fierce dragons, they were harmless.

We really lived without fear of any living creature, and enjoyed the new kinds of plants and animals we found.

Author and Capt. Charlie aboard the Nunoca, 1934

CHAPTER 13

Swashbuckling West Bayer

C aptain Charlie Farrington of West Bay was a big-hearted, exciting man, a non-conformist with a touch of the buccaneer in his soul. He was, however, a rather mild pirate of the swashbuckling type, never cruel, not a robber, but he delighted in flouting authority, and did so whenever the opportunity arose and the circumstances justified it in his opinion. He even looked the part — strong, handsome face, gleaming polished brown skin, snapping black eyes, wavy black hair, broad-muscled shoulders. He was very knowledgeable about his rights, his authority, as master of his ship, and he knew just how far he could go without stepping over the line into trouble.

He was an expert sailor, and his small, two-masted schooner, the *Tuecoi*, about forty-five feet long, with no auxiliary engine, could swiftly skim over the sea as gracefully as a flying fish. She was beautiful to watch.

Cap'n Charlie often did something apparently only to amuse himself, but which usually turned out to the enjoyment or benefit of those he seemed to be using. For instance, to relieve the monotony of long days at sea, he would invite someone to sail with him who could amuse him and his passengers and crew. Uncle Joe Hyde had once been a seaman, but ill-health and advancing age had forced him to give up the sea and live ashore alone in a small shack near Northwest Point. He had no children, and his wife, Disia, had died while he was at sea.

One day Cap'n Charlie appeared at his door. "Come look at de door, Uncle Joe," he called.

"Who dat is?" replied a weak voice.

"Is Cap'n Charlie, Uncle Joe. Come so see de "old wife" I bring you for your supper." He handed the gleaming fish to the old man.

Uncle Joe moved slowly and painfully into the sunshine, and they sat on a bench by the door and chatted. Finally Cap'n Charlie brought up the real reason for his visit.

"Uncle Joe, I wants you come wid me when I go Tampa nex' week."

"No, mon, no. I has to stop at home," came the reply.

"But what do you?"

"Oh, oh, Cap'n, my heart not no good. I took in wid a bad spell Sat'dy gone a week. De nex' one will carry me, true."

"But you not have to do no work, Uncle Joe. Jus' rest, and breathe dat sea air, and sing one little song once in a way for me. It do you good. I fancy dis jus' what you needs. What make you not come wid me?"

With a little more cajoling, Uncle Joe was persuaded to take the trip to Tampa, the only price for passage being "one little song" when he felt like it. He returned several pounds heavier, with sprightlier step, and a smile on his face. It was three years before his bad heart "carried" him.

Another protegé of Cap'n Charlie's was little Berchie Powery. Little Berchie was about twelve years old, but with the body of a scrawny five-year-old, and the wizened brown-skinned face of an old man, sparse blond hair, and sad, hopeless eyes. He may not have been retarded, but he was the butt of ridicule and scorn in his large family. Berchie had not been able to hold his own in the little school, so he had been allowed to stay at home most of the time. He lived in the outlying area of Barkers, in the District of West Bay, in a small, thatch-roofed house, and had never been even to George Town, nine miles away.

One day Cap'n Charlie showed up at Berchie's home, and was met at the door by his mother, Clincy.

"Clincy, I wants you make me take little Berchie wid me when I go Tampa nex' week," he greeted her. Clincy looked in amazement at Cap'n Charlie.

"But no harm, Cap'n Charlie, why you want to take dat nash child— he too fool!"

"No mind, Clincy — he can dance a little jig for me, and give me a laugh now and again."

"Well, if you says so. Berchie gone since soon to look tops for me, so I can plait some baskets. I make him know you wants him to go. T'ank you, Cap'n Charlie; Berchie not been nowhere, no, mon."

And so little Berchie was taken on the great adventure of his life. He ate ravenously, clung to Cap'n Charlie, danced a little jig for everyone's entertainment when asked to, and became the pet of the passengers and crew. He saw the sights of Tampa, including the first and probably only movie of his life, starring Tom Mix. He rode in a taxi and on a street car.

He was dazzled by the neon signs and lights of the city at night, and he went home with his first new clothes and his first pair of shoes, new or second-hand. Berchie had enough adventures to tell about. It made him the center of attention at home and with his few friends for the first time in his life. That trip was only the first of many as Berchie continued sailing for many years.

Cap'n Charlie was the only Caymanian master who set sail when he said he would. Other departing ships dillied

Capt. Charlie Farrington with an aspiring sailor on a trip to Tampa

and dallied, waiting for Earlyn to go tell his Aunt Fadie goodbye, or for Tommy Ebanks, who had not yet left his home at Batabano, nine miles away, or delaying departure for any excuse — or none at all. Everyone knew this and would have considered it most unusual and thoughtless, in fact downright inexcusable, for the vessel to have left earlier than two or three hours after the announced time, which had been passed by word of mouth.

Except where Cap'n Charlie was concerned — if he sent out word he was sailing at 10 o'clock Monday morning, any passenger or cargo not there would be left on the rocks. No exceptions were made: he once left his own father on the dock in George Town.

One bright sunny morning in 1927, the little *Tuecoi* lay at anchor in Hog Stye Bay, George Town, preparing to sail for Nueva Gerona, Isle of Pines. Cap'n Charlie was ashore finishing up business, and the usual crowd was gathered on the landing where the government launch was berthed, and from which the small ship's dory would take passengers out to the *Tuecoi*. Most of the townspeople were on hand as usual for the departure of a ship.

Just across the road was the post office, from which mail was dispatched on any departing vessel, regardless of its destination. Cap'n Charlie had sent word to have the mail bag on the dock by 10:45 A.M. sharp, as he was sailing at 11. At 10:40, he hailed a small boy: "Gladstone, go so tell dem at de post office — I leavin'. Get de mail here."

No one appeared. At 10:50 he condescended — as he was dealing with His Majesty's Service — to send a second message: "Go so tell dem I not waitin' no longer. I gone."

The people watched expectantly, shuffling their feet, grinning, sometimes chuckling. Cap'n Charlie, grinning and waving mischievously, jumped into the loaded dory, cast off, and was pulled out to the *Tuecoi* by two seamen. As the dory drew near to the *Tuecoi*, Mally Coe, a seventeen-year-old lad, came running from the post office lugging the heavy mail sack, and calling, "Cap'n Charlie! Wait! Wait! You can't leave the mail!"

Cap'n Charlie — as my father, who was on board, told us later — threw back his head and laughed while the seamen, caught up in the thrill of the chase, hoisted every inch of sail. The strong wind, perfect for sailing, filled the white sails, and the *Tuecoi* heeled over until the mainsail almost dipped in the brilliant blue water, as she danced over the waves with enough speed to have won the America's Cup. Cap'n Charlie stood on the deck, head thrown back, chortling as he watched Mally in the gasoline launch fall hopelessly behind. "But how he t'ink he could have catch me?" he demanded, as Mally finally abandoned the chase and returned to the dock, making his way with hanging head through the laughing crowd.

There is a sequel to the tale — Cap'n Charlie always stopped in West Bay to tell his wife and family goodbye, so the postmaster commandeered a car and drove the seven miles to West Bay, delivering the mail to the ship while Cap'n Charlie was ashore. The mail did get through.

Several years later, after his beloved *Tuecoi* had been mashed on the rocks during a storm, Cap'n Charlie became master of the *Nunoca*, a long, narrow motor ship modelled after her predecessor, the *Noca*, a converted sub chaser. His regular run was from George Town to Tampa, Florida, stopping each way at the Isle of Pines.

He had little patience with or tolerance for Cubans in general, and even less for Cuban soldiers, and he welcomed any opportunity to thumb his nose at them and get away with it.

"Land Ahoy," sailor aboard the Tuecoi

He did a little good-hearted smuggling of gasoline and American cigarettes and such when he came from Tampa to the Isle of Pines, for the duty on such items made the prices very high. I was on board once as the *Nunoca* sailed slowly up the winding river to Nueva Gerona; Cap'n Charlie gave orders to bring three drums of gasoline and a few packages on deck. I watched curiously, wondering what was going on, as a small gasoline launch came out of the mangroves along the banks and eased alongside. The drums and packages were quickly lowered, and the boat headed back into the mangroves and disappeared, with very few words having been exchanged, as the *Nunoca* continued up the river. This kind of operation was repeated on each trip. He made no money on the deals — he just enjoyed outwitting the Cuban authorities while doing a favor for friends.

The incident that he seemed to have enjoyed with the most gusto occurred when his ship was in port and a prisoner had escaped from the Cuban penitentiary in the Isle of Pines. He told me the story a year or so after it happened. Cuban soldiers were searching every vessel before it was allowed to depart. It galled Cap'n Charlie to have to allow Cuban soldiers on board his ship, but he complied, warning the men, "I gone in fifteen minutes. You mus' get off my ship by den, I tellin' you."

Fifteen minutes passed, and no soldiers appeared on deck. Cap'n Charlie sent a seaman below to tell the soldiers to get off the ship immediately. When he had waited the bare minimum of time he felt he could, he gave orders to the engineer to start the engine, and to the seamen to cast off, and the *Nunoca* pulled away from the dock.

The soldiers, who had been taking their time searching the hold, pounded up the companionway onto the deck, arrogantly ordering Cap'n Charlie to put back and let them go ashore. Cap'n Charlie, hiding his glee as best he could, said, "I dam' if I put back — jump off, mon, and swim back, I telling you."

The soldiers stamped their feet, waved their arms, swore great Spanish oaths, and one started to pull his gun. Cap'n Charlie looked him in the eye, "You can't scare me wid dat," he told the man scornfully.

The soldiers continued their demands, while Cap'n Charlie calmly watched them and remained firm. "I not takin' unna back, no, mon." However, after letting them rant for awhile, he told them there was a gun boat at the mouth of the river, and they could jump off onto it as the *Nunoca* cruised past. The soldiers refused angrily, upon which Cap'n Charlie gave them his ultimatum, "You get off my wessel at de mout' of de river or you go Tampa wid me. Dat all I got to say," and he turned his back on them.

Finally realizing they could not intimidate Cap'n Charlie, and that they were fast approaching the gun boat, the soldiers agreed to the transfer. They jumped to the deck of the gunboat as the *Nunoca* slowed down and eased up beside her, but threaten Cap'n Charlie with predictions of what the authorities would do to him when he next returned to Nueva Gerona.

An American passenger had watched the altercation with great interest. "If the gun boat had not been here, or if the soldiers had continued to refuse, what would you really have done?"

Cap'n Charlie, laughingly replied, "I'd have took dem all de way to Tampa, true!" And he waved jauntily and merrily to the angry and disgruntled soldiers.

The sequel to this story was that when Cap'n Charlie returned to Nueva Gerona, not only did he not get into trouble with the authorities, but he learned that the soldiers had been put in jail for three months for disobeying his orders to get off his ship.

Cap'n Charlie not only was a most competent man of the sea, but he also had charm, a sense of humor, compassion, courage, and good sense. He was a delight to know, and to remember. No one has ever quite taken his place.

George Merren and Rose Arch on their wedding day

CHAPTER 14

Spoken For

D ating or going steady did not occur in Cayman while we lived there. When Limeon would "come to look for" Whynona, her father (if he was on the island) or her mother would greet him with "What are your intentions?" Of course he had to declare honorable intentions, that is marriage, if he didn't want to be turned from the door then and there. If Whynona accepted his attentions, they were considered engaged.

With engagement being the first step in courtship, the consequence was many broken engagements, as well as engagements that continued for years. The engagement was acknowledged by "Limeon is running Whynona," or "Whynona is spoken for."

Because most women stayed on the island while the men went to sea or away to work ashore in the United States, Jamaica, Cuba, or Central America, a couple would become engaged while the man was home for a short time. It would then be at least a year and sometimes several years before he would return, at which time they would continue the engagement, get married, or break up.

Even with the engagement, there was none of the dating as we experience it. This was mostly because there were few places to go, but also because it was not considered proper for even an engaged couple to spend much time alone.

When a young man called on his fianceé, they could sit and visit in the parlor, or in a porch swing, or go for a walk or bicycle ride. They could attend the occasional dance, party, or beach picnic, or go to church. Sometimes moonlight sails were organized on a small schooner which happened to be in port, or had just been launched. Romance was a moonlight sail over a smooth sea, when boys and girls could sit close to each other, holding hands and even sometimes catching a chance to hug or kiss, and singing "Moonlight Bay" or "Pagan Love Song."

Although, as I have said, we girls and boys did not really date — we still felt the same attractions as teenagers anywhere. I had not been on the island very long when I "fell" for a very attractive boy, and the feeling seemed to be mutual. The first time I remember seeing Otto was at a picnic and swimming party at Smith's Barcadere. When I arrived with my friends, he was already there, but was not in the sea. He was sitting up on the ironshore watching those in the water. I don't know when he first noticed me, or if he had seen me somewhere before, but I hadn't been in the sea very long before he began pelting me with little bits of harmless twigs or shells. It didn't take that to get my attention — I had already picked him out as someone special, but of course I tried to appear indifferent.

From that day on, until we left the island nearly three years later, I enjoyed a full-fledged case of puppy love. I knew all the time, of course, that it would have to come to an end when we returned to the States, but that seemed very far in the future, particularly because we didn't know how long we would be there.

And so we enjoyed each other's company whenever we could get together — on bicycle rides, walks to the beach in a group singing "Side by Side." On moonlight picnics, while playing ring games, I could depend on him to pick me from the circle and thus get a peck on the cheek.

I had never had the opportunity to learn to ride a bicycle, so Otto offered to teach me to ride on his sister's bike. He would hold up the bike while I got on, then steady me by holding the back of the seat, and running along beside me. That had to be real devotion to do that in the hot afternoon sun. That was so pleasant for me that it took me longer than it should have to be able to ride on my own, and even then I couldn't seem to get the hang of mounting and getting off without aid. Otto would hold me up and start me off, then when we planned to stop, he would ride ahead and hold me up while I dismounted! However, my pride took over, and before too long I was riding along with Otto and the rest on the bicycle that my parents got me for my birthday.

Once in a while I would get a little moody or blue for some reason, but all it would take was just the sight of Otto passing by to bring out the sunshine again. I remember well the Christmas morning when we passed his home on our way to church, and he was standing on the front steps proudly wearing his first pair of long pants.

When the time eventually came for us to return home to the States, it was hard to say goodbye. We kept in touch by letter for several years. I treasure the memories of that innocent and guileless association.

A happy group of young people aboard the Nunoca, 1934

In spite of my young age and relative innocence, I soon became aware that actual practice varied quite widely from the expressed moral standards, as it was quite apparent that pregnancy outside of marriage as well as pregnancy before marriage was fairly common. I heard of one young man who said he wanted to be sure his fianceé could bear children, so he made certain of this before the wedding took place.

Pregnancies outside of marriage resulted in many single mothers having to make a living for themselves and their child or children with no help from the father, who was married to someone else, or who refused to accept responsibility. The identity of the father was usually known, and sometimes he would acknowledge the child and provide for it. Two terms for illegitimate babies were "outside child" and "bush baby." As I understood it, "outside child" was more respectable, "bush baby" having the connotation of promiscuity. There seemed to be little if any ostracism of either the child or the mother after the event occurred.

No couples attempted to keep a marriage secret, and it was almost impossible for an elopement to occur, for banns had to be read from the pulpit seven days before the wedding date. However, as there was little visiting from one settlement to another, sometimes a couple would succeed in a surprise marriage by publishing the banns and marrying in Bodden Town, for instance, although the bride lived in George Town. It was also possible sometimes for couples to obtain a special license that did not require banns. Both these practices were to circumvent strong parental objection to the match.

Lina Jackson of Newlands and Hughie Jackson of Savannah had their banns read in George Town without the news reaching her Aunt Lina and Uncle Farrell, with whom she lived in Newlands. She went to George Town ostensibly to stay a few days with our family. My mother made her a dress for her wedding, and they were married at the Presbyterian manse. (My father, although he was a minister, had not been able to obtain a license to perform marriages.) Arthur Bodden had been hired to take them to Newlands after the ceremony, which he did, blowing his horn all the way. I was allowed to ride along, and when we got to the end of the road, from where we had to walk about a quarter of a mile to the house, Lina had me run ahead to break the news to Aunt Lina, which, of course, made me feel very important. This wedding was unusual in its simplicity.

Weddings were usually big social events, with months of preparation. The bride had to have a trousseau, including the wedding dress, a second dress, a going-away dress (even though she might not be going anywhere!), lingerie, bed and table linens, etc. As most engagements were long, she had plenty of time to assemble all these in her hope chest. However, sometimes the prospective groom would purchase most of the clothes, including the wedding dress, in the States and bring them home with him. If this was not the case, the dresses and lingerie would be made by a dressmaker or a member of the family, as ready-to-wear clothes were not available on the island. (One exception to this was hats; Merrens had a small millinery shop next to the larger general store, where they did a thriving business. Everyday hats were hand-woven from thatch palm, and were bought from the maker for a shilling or two.) House linens were lovingly and beautifully hand-made, embroidered, and decorated with crochet by the bride and her friends or family members.

The bridal party was made up of anywhere from three to ten bridesmaids and male attendants, a flower girl, a ring bearer, and sometimes junior bridesmaids (little girls). The girls' dresses were elaborate; the men usually wore dark suits, sometimes with black bow ties.

A sit-down dinner-reception at the home of the bride followed the wedding, the size and elaborateness determined by the social and financial situation of the families involved. I handpainted place cards for one of the Merren wedding dinners.

Honeymoon trips were virtually unknown. Occasionally the groom would take his bride back to the States or wherever he was working, but as

Waiting to be "Spoken for"

most of them were seamen, the brides usually remained on the island, raising their families and seeing their husbands only on their rare visits home.

Women tended to accept separations from their husbands and marital infidelity as facts of life which they could not change. They were almost completely dependent on their husbands (or if unmarried, on family members), as there were few opportunities for them to earn money. They stayed at home, worked hard, and raised their children without complaint.

Miss Ella Hurlston dressed for an outing.

However, sometimes the burden became too great, either because of finances, or because the mother didn't feel she had the strength to take care of all her children. Therefore, it was quite common for a child to be raised by other than its birth parents, although no one seemed to even think of formal, legal adoption. Sometimes an unmarried mother would give her child to someone else, but often married parents would give their child to a couple who had no children, or to a family that needed more help. Contact with the birth family was continued, although most if not all of the needs of the child were met by the "foster" parents. Doris and Janey, two sisters about six and eight years old, came to our house frequently, backing baskets of provisions such as bananas, limes, cassava, and so forth, for sale. Mother usually bought something from them. One day their mother came with them, and announced to my mother that she was giving her Doris and Janey. Mother was flabbergasted, but also touched, and wished that she could accept the gift, but she declined as graciously as she could, hoping not to hurt anyone's feelings. I often imagined what a sensation it would have been for us to have shown up at home in Mississippi with Doris and Janey as my little sisters! I think we always looked on the two little girls with extra fondness after that.

Someone later told Mother (I can't of course vouch for the truth of it) that this mother was quite ingenious in providing for her children: she would "give" them to some family, then after a few months, when they had been provided with clothes, etc., she would reclaim them.

If any divorce occurred while we were in Cayman, I was not aware of it. I don't recall ever hearing divorce mentioned. I knew there were women whose husbands had not been heard from for long periods of time, and families that seemed to have been deserted, but women tended to accept these situations with resignation. The alternatives, which I figured out even then, were to be a single woman with no children or husband, dependent on other family members, or to be a single mother with no means to care for her children and no government social programs to help out.

It was not an easy life, but Caymanians — men, women, and children — managed to meet life and its problems and hardships with equanimity and serenity.

The launching of the Cimboco in 1927 was a festive event.

CHAPTER 15

Walk Away With the Rope Now!

L aunching a schooner was one of the big social events in Cayman, in which everyone, regardless of financial or social standing, could, and was encouraged to, participate. When a ship was ready for launching, the word would go out. The announcement was understood by all to be an invitation for everyone to come — and they did. The owners of the ship provided bountiful amounts of food — turtle stew, rice-and-peas, fried plantain, heavy cake, conch stew, and other native delicacies. They also hired a fiddler at least, but more often a band made up of a fiddler, a drummer on a home-made drum, a man rattling bones, and someone producing rhythm with a kitchen fork on a grater to provide entertainment throughout the day. Liquor was also provided, and flowed freely, so that drunken brawls sometimes broke out — also part of the entertainment for the crowd! Everyone was expected to join in pulling (it was considered good luck to have women pull). The ship was literally pulled into the sea by hand.

A heavy line was run through a "block" (type of pulley) anchored to a piece of coral out in the sea from the spot on shore where the launching took place, and attached to the bow of the ship. At the given signal, men, women, and children, most dressed in new clothes, and most women wearing hats, grabbed the hawser, and followed commands: "Man your falls! All hands! . . . Walk away! Walk away back! . . . Walk away back with the rope now! Comin' home! Walk away! . . . She's two blocks now! Whoa!" And the block would be repositioned by men who waded or swam out in the sea. As this required time, everyone took the chance to rest, eat, drink, dance to the fiddle, and visit with friends. Then back to pulling, accompanied by sea chanteys, such as "O Miss Louisiana."

This process continued throughout the day until the ship, with much scraping and groaning and amid wild cheering, finally plunged into the sea, sending up cascades of water. As she slid in, a pretty girl christened her by

Capt. Rayal Bodden, shipbuilder and architect (center), with Hilary Conrad (left), and an unidentified young onlooker.

Launching of the Lady Slater at Capt. Rayal Bodden's shipyard on North Church Street

smashing against her stern a bottle of what might have been champagne wrapped in burlap to hold in the fragments of glass, and intoning the plea, "From rocks and seas in foreign lands, may God protect the *Cimboco* (or whatever ship)."

In truth, the rocks on Cayman's shores posed as much of a danger as those in foreign lands. Ships in port during a storm were sometimes "mashed on the rocks." To avoid this, masters sailed their ships to safety in North Sound if there was time.

Ships were launched to Cayman rhythms.

On following days the builders finished up the necessary work, sometimes waiting to set the masts after launching. When all was completed, she "got her sails on" and was ready for her maiden voyage.

Sometimes a group of people from one district would make an all-day excursion to a launching on another part of the island. About twenty of us from George Town, including George Allan England, an American travel writer and his wife, Blanche, packed picnic lunches, hired a motorboat, and went all the way through North Sound and around to North Side for a launching. That was the only time in three years of living without refrigeration of any kind that we fell victim to food poisoning. Practically everyone spent a night of vomiting and diarrhea, but we all recovered without any more serious symptoms, and without any medical attention.

The launching of the *Cimboco* (Cayman Island Motor Boat Company) in 1927 was an especially festive occasion, as it was the first time a motor ship had been built on the island. In fact, the Colonial Report for the year stated: "The only circumstance of local moment . . . was . . . the building of a motor-vessel by a local company . . . and the initiation of a regular service . . ." A few years later, a second motor ship, the *Lady Slater*, was launched. Captain Rayal Bodden built both in his shipyard located on the waterfront north of the center of George Town. The *Cimboco* carried freight, passengers, and mail, making fifteen voyages a year to Jamaica and three to an American port.

An interesting and to us amazing incident occurred when the *Cimboco* was ready for her engine, which was being shipped to Kingston, Jamaica, from Scotland, I think it was, or England. When word came that it was in Kingston, a race was on to see which schooner would get to bring it to Cayman. This was a prize cargo, bringing good income and prestige.

I am not sure of the ships involved, and have found no one who remembers, but, according to Elroy Arch, they could have been the *Express*, Panton Thompson, master, and the *Fulmar*, Gerald Coe, master, as these two were on the Jamaica run at the time. The two vessels set out on the same day, and everyone was full of speculation as to which one would reach Kingston first and secure the prize.

About nine or ten days later, "Sa-a-i-l ho-o-o!" rang out on the George Town waterfront. The sail spotted was so tiny that my parents and I could barely see it, yet the expert watchers proclaimed, "Yas, dat be de *Fulmar*. She got de motor, she has."

"But how Cap'n Gerald get dere forst?" someone wondered. After only a few moments of consultation among the group of men came the answer,

"Cap'n Gerald, he smart. He not go Kingston forst, he put in at Sav-la-Mar, hire a car take him to Montpelier, and he take de train to Kingston and beat Cap'n Panton. Yas, mon, dat what he do, true."

All that from peering at the small dot on the horizon. We had been in Cayman long enough to not be surprised when the passengers and crew of the *Fulmar* came ashore and confirmed that that was exactly what had occurred.

Crewmen at work

CHAPTER 16

Mutiny on the *Explicit*

T he most exciting experience of my life up to that time occurred on a trip to Jamaica on the three-master *Explicit,* a wind-jammer. It was another highlight of my years in Cayman.

My mother and father and I were ready for a trip somewhere, and Jamaica seemed a good choice. But money was a problem. The schooner that made regular trips to Jamaica from Cayman charged two pounds ten shillings ($13.00) one way, so that was out of our reach. We didn't even consider the luxury of taking passage on the *Cimboco,* the new motor ship which had just been launched, and was making regular trips to Kingston, for passage on her was four pounds ($20.00) one way. My father then thought of the *Explicit,* and when it came in shortly after we began trying to make plans, Daddy talked to Captain Ritch, and came home jubilant: Captain Ritch had agreed to take us for one pound ten shillings ($7.50) each. That amount we were sure we could manage, and still have some money for expenses ashore. We excitedly began making plans to travel on the *Explicit* on her next trip.

Because of rough seas at George Town, we had to go by car to Bodden Town, where we boarded the *Explicit* about 3 o'clock on Friday, March 4, 1927. Because of the reef, the ship had to anchor a long way out, and because of low tide, even a small boat could not get clear in to shore. The seamen solved that problem by picking us up and carrying us out to the small boat, which transported us out to the ship.

The trip was already exciting for me, but soon became more so. Our relatives in Mobile had missed the ship on its trip before Christmas, and so had sent all our Christmas gifts on this trip. We had great fun opening all the packages, and managed to get through them and eat some apples (what a treat!) that Captain Ritch had given us before the rough sea laid us low.

Rough seas and headwinds prevented our reaching Little Cayman (a distance of about seventy miles) until Sunday afternoon the sixth, where we unloaded cargo. According to my diary, it was about noon the next day before we anchored at Cayman Brac, the distance to our anchorage being about twelve miles, although the shortest distance between the two islands was only five miles. Cayman Brac was Captain Ritch's home, so we spent the night ashore. My diary says, "His wife and everybody is very nice to us."

I don't remember where my parents stayed (probably with the Ritches) but I stayed with a girl named Lynn Foster, who had never even heard of me before, but who treated me like a dear friend, so much so that she offered me the use of her toothbrush as I had left mine on board! She took me up on the Bluff the next morning, and I also had the opportunity to take a good bath and wash my hair before we set sail that afternoon for Jamaica. Captain Ritch's wife and their two small children joined us for the voyage, and their

"Calm before the Storm," Jamaica bound aboard the Explicit

son Callan, a shy teen-ager, was already on the ship as a member of the crew.

Favorable winds over smooth seas got us to Savannah-la-Mar by Friday, March 11. When we went on deck early that morning we saw a most spectacular sunrise over the mountains. Several of the seamen, including the cook, went ashore, and we managed to squeeze into a boat going ashore. Meanwhile, preparations began on board to unload a deck load of lumber.

Soon after we returned to the ship and the unloading began, it became apparent that all the seamen, including Captain Ritch's nephew who was his first mate, were drunk. The men were pitching lumber down to a lighter with several Jamaican men on it, and were doing it so roughly that it was dangerous. When Captain Ritch began reprimanding them, things got nasty.

I remember standing with the other passengers on the foredeck watching the proceedings when, after a sharp order from the captain to be more careful, one of the seamen defiantly confronted him. Captain Ritch immediately with one blow knocked him off the pile of lumber he was standing on to the deck, blood streaming from his nose.

The rest of the men, including the mate, refused to continue work, and knotted in a muttering group aft. Captain Ritch ordered all of us passengers to remain on the foredeck or in the cabins below, while he dealt with the situation.

I don't remember feeling frightened, just very excited—here I was, a spectator to a real live mutiny! After about an hour, we began to get hungry, but the cook was drunk, and besides, the galley was in "enemy territory" and we had no food. One of the passengers was a girl who had a cousin among the seamen, so Captain Ritch agreed to let her go to the galley and bring back whatever she could find for our lunch. She carried out her mission with no trouble from the mutineers, and we happily made a feast of mangoes, bananas, oranges, cheese and biscuits.

In another hour or two, the men were sobering up, and went back to work unloading the lumber, with care for the workers on the lighter. When the unloading was finished, Captain Ritch immediately fired all of those, including his nephew, who had been involved in the mutiny. He paid them off, and put them ashore in Sav-La-Mar. We still had the cook, however, he hadn't mutinied, he'd just gotten drunk. Three or four other seamen had not been involved, so with this skeleton crew, Captain Ritch sailed on to Montego Bay, where he hired Jamaican seamen to complete the voyage.

Christmas colours: White sand yards and pink conch shells

CHAPTER 17

White Sand Christmas

C hristmas is coming!" — magic words to a twelve-year-old to whom Christmas had always been very special. The lack of snow was no problem, as we had lived in the southern part of the United States since I was six years old. However, the lack of Christmas trees was a serious problem. I had never experienced a Christmas without a tree of some kind, even though there had often been few gifts.

Mother and Daddy knew that a tree had to be found some way. Nothing we could see fit the image of a Christmas tree, even remotely. In desperation they consulted with Leighton Bush, an elder in our church. He probably could not even visualize what they wanted, but he cheerfully led them into the bush to hunt for something. Evergreens were non-existent, but they finally came back with a five-foot bush with very small leaves, which Daddy set up in a bay window in the living room. That was a logical place, of course, but nevertheless it was a big mistake. In a few hours the tiny leaves were curling up, and the light beaming through the windows behind the tree emphasized its lack of beauty.

We had not brought any ornaments, and none were available at any store. A friend in the Isle of Pines had sent us a box of chocolate candies wrapped in bright red, blue, green, or gold foil. I carefully smoothed out each piece of foil and covered cones from one of the two casuarina (Australian pine) trees in George Town. Then I went to Merren's store and bought inexpensive metallic ribbon in several colors. I wanted to have some sort of gift for people who came to see us, so I cut the ribbon in six-inch lengths, and printed "Merry Christmas" in India ink on each one. These I hung on the tree, and presented each visitor with a bookmark, which was surely one of the most inappropriate gifts most of them had ever received, but which they graciously accepted.

I have a clearer picture of that scrawny little tree in my mind than of any other tree in my life, not because it was in the least pretty, but because it represented giving in love. For the next two Christmases we spent in Cayman, we fared a little better for trees. Daddy was able to get some branches from an Australian pine and tie them together to make a tree that didn't wilt immediately. In fact, they kept quite well, even though their shape was decidedly unorthodox.

For our little American family, Christmas often continued for weeks afterward until all our gifts from the States arrived. One year we received our last gifts on the *Explicit* from Mobile in March.

A white Christmas in Cayman meant snow-white yards. One of the first acts of preparation for Christmas was "backing sand." Several weeks before the holidays, on a moonlit night, a mother would call out, "Come so! We go back sand tonight." The word would spread to nearby households, and soon a jolly, laughing group, made up mostly of women and children, each carrying a hand-made thatch basket with long strap handles, would head for the nearest beach. They scooped sand into each basket, then lifted it to their back, with the strap coming over their shoulders, where it was either placed over the forehead to bear the weight, or over crossed wrists. It amazed me how much weight could be carried that way, even by fairly small children.

When they reached home, they emptied each basket of sand into a pile by itself, spacing the piles evenly about the yard. Just before Christmas Day, women and children spread the sand smoothly over the yard, sweeping it into intricate patterns with twig brooms. (Yards were kept cleanly swept all the time, the women even sweeping the road in front of the house.) The men meantime collected fresh conch shells, which they lined up on each side of the walk to the front door. The glistening white sand, the pink, lavender, and yellow shells, and the richly variegated croton bushes around the house and yard blended into a truly festive sight for the holidays. These decorations cost no money, only time and labor that was turned into fun.

Two or three weeks before Christmas, "marching" began. Bands of people strolled from house to house at night, singing — but not Christmas carols, just whatever the popular songs were at that time. They would be given food or drink (often rum or something similar, or non-alcoholic "syrup"), sometimes cigarettes, at each house, so as the evening and the marching went on, boisterous hilarity broke out frequently among the groups that consumed the alcoholic drinks. Of course, I was allowed to go only with those who did not accept drinks stronger than "strawberry syrup."

It was common for stores to set up special sales of novelty items. We lived next door to the H. O. Merren Store on Shedden Road, which was the

Ruth and Clayton Merren holding a Christmas sale, 1926

largest shop in the Cayman Islands at that time. Orrie Merren got my parents' permission to put up counters made of planks laid across sawhorses in our yard, under the star apple tree. Two or three of the Merren daughters, two or three cousins, and I were hired to sell noise makers, fireworks, "googly-eye" glasses, and other carnival-type merchandise. The sale lasted several days. We had a great time, and sold out almost all of the items.

Meantime, the store was busy selling hats and shoes and material for the new clothes everyone had to have. With no distinct change of seasons, Christmas marked the time for new apparel. In Cayman it was the "Christmas Parade" rather than the Easter Parade, as everyone walked to church, the girls and women in new hats, new shoes, and new dresses. Until adolescence, boys wore knee pants, so when a boy finally got his first long

Children helping to 'sand down the yard' — "backing" fresh sand from the beach.

pants, it was often at Christmas, and men sported new white suits, made by local seamstresses.

In Cayman, as elsewhere, food was an important part of the celebrations. Women spent days preparing special foods, especially rich, dark, rum-laced fruitcake and heavy cake. Turkeys were unknown, but there was extra butchering of beef or turtles. The meat was cooked into rich, dark stews, seasoned highly with hot peppers containing chunks of cassava, yam, coco, plantain, or pumpkin.

In addition to concerts, often held around Christmas as already mentioned, cake sales were a popular means of making money for churches, and many of these were also held around Christmas, even on Christmas Eve. Our church used our yard for our sales, all cake sales being held outside. Not only were cakes, homemade ice cream, candy, and other food items sold, but also handmade gift items, such as crocheted sisal hats, mats, and purses. We introduced some types of games as well, such as a fortune wheel and a fish pond, but my mother and father made sure that these were not to be seen as types of gambling. The fortune wheel rewarded players with prizes, everyone getting at least a piece of candy, but some winning a handkerchief, a bottle of perfume, or some trinket. Every "fisherman" was assured some sort of catch, even if he or she had to be given a little help. My diary records that at one Christmas Eve sale the fortune wheel (which I was in charge of) took in over a pound, equivalent to about $5.00. At thruppence (three pennies) a spin, that seemed like big money to me.

The most important event of Christmas was the service held in each church on Christmas morning, regardless of the day of the week on which Christmas occurred. No church would have considered omitting the Christmas Day service. A Christmas program featuring the children, but involving adults as well, was also usually presented sometime around Christmas.

Caymanian men working abroad or at sea tried to include Christmas in their leave time, and all Caymanian schooners tried to make it home for Christmas. I recorded in my diary:

"Wed.: When we got up this morning, the *Drew* was anchored in the harbor . . . The *Gold Medal* came this afternoon.

Sun.: *Diamond* came in.

Tues.: The *Resolution* came this morning.

Sun.: We woke up before daybreak and heard "Sail ho." We went back to sleep, and found out this morning when we got up it was the *Fulmar*.

Thurs. Dec. 21: Five boats came in today. The *Arbutus, Sturdee, Wembly*, the *Banks*, and a steamer. *Lady Antoinette* and *Vita* and *Panama* are expected soon."

It was an exciting time as mail arrived, and brothers, sons, sweethearts and husbands returned to their families. Cayman joyfully celebrated the most festive time of the year for a total of three or four weeks.

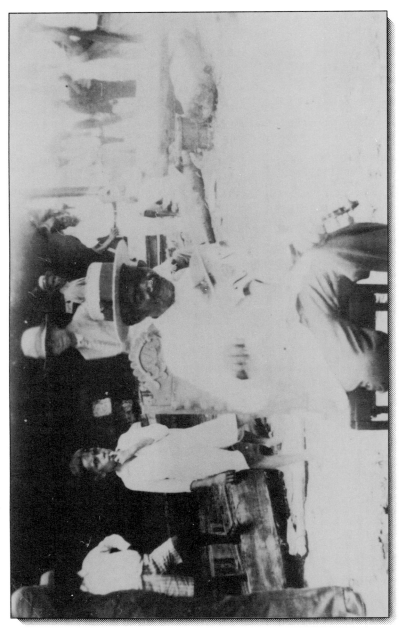

Music of an "enchanted time" still echoes in memory.

Conclusion

Whenat last the time came for us to leave our little island, I was excited of course at going back to the States, but I also felt great sadness. I did not know if I would ever again visit my friends and this place, which had become my home. However, as I could not accept such a prospect, I insisted that I would return, although few people, if any, believed me. Five years later, having held on to my dream, I returned, and spent over three months in Cayman, before my marriage.

In the last twenty-five years, circumstances have made it possible for me to spend much time in Cayman, where I still feel more at home than in any other place where I have formerly lived. Of course, many changes have occurred, but I hope this record will serve to keep alive in memory the simple, unsophisticated period of time, when children, young people, and adults made their own entertainment, welcoming every opportunity to lighten the tedium of life, when crime was almost non-existent, and when life proceeded at a leisurely pace.

So I have shared my memories of the Cayman of my early adolescent years, still vivid in memory, as an almost enchanted isle of carefree happiness. Cayman is a part of me.

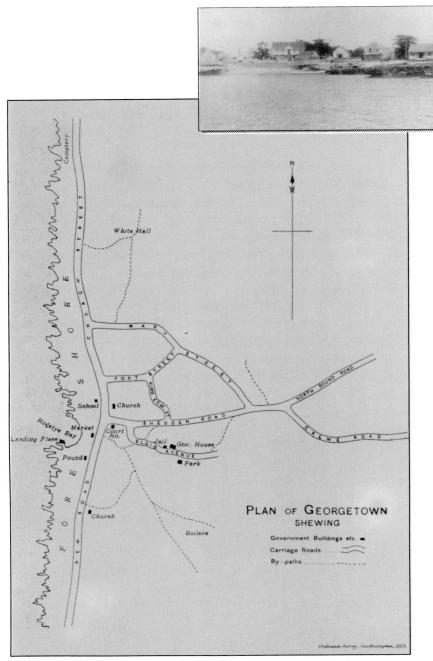

*As predicted by Mrs. Booker, the Islands she knew have
undergone major changes over the last 65 years.*

Appendix

The following material is taken from an article, "A Trip to Southern Isles," by my mother, Frances C. Booker, appearing in *Autumn Leaves*, a church publication, June, 1928. Her foresight seems astonishing, considering the conditions on the island at the time, and her lack of expertise in matters of tourism, business, and industry.

"It is really surprising how many automobiles are on the island. Just in the last few months new ones have been brought in, and they continue to come on almost every boat from Tampa. [She makes a later mention of "from Fords to Cadillacs."] This will necessarily bring about an improvement in the roads and the opening up of others. I predict that within a few years East End and North Side can be reached by car, and that will be a great benefit to the people.

There is talk very frequently of a wireless station, and that will come, too, for once the demand is felt people will not be long setting about to supply that demand. Just recently there has been installed an oil and gas station, and I hear that there is a movement on foot to erect a larger ice plant, sufficient to meet the demands and needs of the island. I am of the opinion, too, that ere a great while an electric plant will be furnishing light. Within recent months one sees the soft, clear glow of the Aladdin lamp from many of the homes; this is rapidly taking the place of the ordinary oil lamp. There are also quite a number of gas lights in use and one Delco lighting system. One surely sees that Cayman's light is increasing, and I think it presages the dawn of a new and brighter day. At present time there is no hotel, but with the progress made in other directions, and with the increasing demand that will be forthcoming, Cayman should get her share of the tourist trade to these southern isles. For those who desire a quiet, restful place to spend a vacation, Cayman should be quite to their liking."

Agouti: A rabbit sized rodent native to South and Central America and to the Caribbean. It looks like a large, long-legged guinea-pig.

Aloes (Aloe Vera): A succulent perennial of the lily family and is highly regarded as a medicinal plant in the tropics.

Asafetida: A bitter fetid gum resin with an unpleasant onion-like smell, obtained from the roots of various oriental plants; used in folk medicine.

Backing: A verb, meaning to carry a load on one's back.

Banns: The public announcement of a proposed marriage.

Biscuit: A small hard or crisp dry baked cracker or cookie.

Bottler: A cooking banana — a cross between a plantain and a banana.

Bow: The forward end or part of a vessel.

Breadfruit: A large green fruit. The starchy fibrous pulp is used as a vegetable. It can only be eaten cooked.

Breadkind: Any starchy food either raw or cooked, such as breadfruit, cassava, coco, yam, sweet potato, etc.

Bush: Any uncleared areas with shrubs and trees.

Caboose: A wooden box on legs, filled with sand in which a fire is made for cooking.

Cassava: A woody flowering shrub with large edible, starchy root tubers.

Cat Boat: A double ended vessel, averaging between 13 to 16 feet and chiefly used for pursuing turtles.

Cerassee: A climbing vine of the cucumber and pumpkin family. Its leaves are boiled to make a tea used for a wide variety of ailments.

Coco: A white, starchy, edible root used especially in soups.

Cookrum (Cookroom): The traditional separate kitchen located some distance behind the house.

Crawl: An enclosed pen made of mangrove pilings. Built in shallow, coastal water to contain turtle, etc.

Croton: A decorative shrub of the South Pacific with leaves of many interesting shapes, patterns and colour variations.

Fathom: A unit of length equal to six feet, used to measure depth of water and length of rope.

Forecastle: The part of the vessel at the bow where the crew is quartered and stores, etc. may be stowed.

Fu-fu (fool-fool): Used to describe someone who is considered slightly crazy, stupid or feeble-minded.

Guinea: A British coin worth 21 shillings.

Guinep: A large shade tree, bearing clusters of small green-skinned fruit.

Heavy cake: A thick moist, pudding-like cake extremely sweet and rich. Made from starchy vegetables and sugar/molasses, coconut milk and butter.

Horse eye: A large flat brown bean which grows on a vine near the sea. Also known as sea chestnut.

Indian Head: Brightly coloured cotton material.

Iguana: A large (some may reach 6.5 feet) and extremely diverse family of lizards that live in warm areas of the Eastern and Western hemispheres.

Leeward: A nautical term describing the point or quarter towards which the wind blows.

Lighter: A large open barge used for transporting cargo, especially in loading or unloading a ship.

Make: To let or permit.

Mangrove: Several species of trees which are commonly found around tropical and sub-tropical coastlines and marshy areas.

Marl: A fine-grained sedimentary rock consisting of clay minerals, calcite or aragonite, and silt.

Nash: Puny, over protected or coddled.

Old wife: A queen trigger fish.

Penny (pl. pennies or pence): A British bronze or copper coin having a value equal to one twelfth of a shilling. Equal to U.S. two cents in 1925.

Plantain: The big brother of the banana family. Plaintains are never eaten raw. This vegetable can be cooked when either green or ripe.

Plantation: A small piece of tilled ground which has been laboriously cleared from the "bush" with a machete. This small area would have been cultivated with "ground provisions".

Obeah: A phenomena of the supernatural, a peculiar form of witchcraft or sorcery, a mild form of voodoo. It was brought to the Caribbean from West Africa during the slave trade.

Pound (pound sterling): The standard monetary unit of the United Kingdom and its dependencies. In 1925, it was equal to U.S. $4.80.

Pumpkin: A large spherical fruit produced by vine-like plants belonging to the gourd family. It is not the American pumpkin. It is usually boiled and used as an ingredient in many dishes.

Red ocher: Any of various natural red earths containing ferric oxide; used as pigments.

Sea egg (sea urchin): Globular marine invertebrate enclosed in a thin brittle shell covered (armed) with movable spines. Found in shallow tropical waters.

Shilling: A British silver coin equal to twelve pennies. In 1925, it was worth U.S. twenty-four cents.

Shaddock: A type of citrus fruit native to Polynesia and Southeast Asia; said to have been brought to Jamaica in the 17th century by a Captain Shaddock. This pink-fleshed fruit with a thick rind is the parent of the modern grapefruit.

Sisal: A strong durable white fiber made from the large fleshly leaves of the agave plant.

Tamarind: A large tree with a dense foliage, native to Southeast Asia, which bears long segmented pods. Each mature segment can be broken to reveal a pulp-covered seed. The pulp has a very sharp, sour and sweet taste.

Thatch: Material from the silver thatch palm, used for roofing, and making baskets, hats and rope.

Three-master: Schooner with three masts.

Tops: Unopened leaves from thatch palms used in making rope, etc.

Unna: Plural form of "you".

Wattle and daub: Building technique of weaving strips of wood (wattles) around standing posts, then plastering with a lime daub made by burning coral in a kiln.

Whelks: A large edible marine snail having a thick-lipped spiral shell; found along the rocky shore line.

White lime: Coral burnt in a lime kiln to fine powder and then mixed with sand into a daub which hardens like concrete.

Windjammer: A large merchant sailing ship.

Yam: A large, edible, hairy tuber with dark brown skin. The starchy flesh may range in hues from pristine white to slightly purple.

About the Author

Aarona Booker Kohlman was born July 7, 1913, in Wellston, Ohio, to N. L. and Frances Cochran Booker. Her father was a missionary for the Reorganized Church of Jesus Christ of Latter Day Saints, and his assignments took him to many places. By the time Aarona was twelve years old, she had lived in Utah, Idaho, several towns and her grandfather's farm in Mississippi, and had not attended a full year at any one school.

When she was twelve years old, her father was assigned to work in the Isle of Pines and Grand Cayman. After nearly three years, he was reassigned, and the family returned to the United States in the summer of 1928.

Aarona graduated in 1930 at the age of sixteen from the same school she had started in Vancleave, Mississippi. She enrolled in Graceland College, Lamoni, Iowa, that fall, and graduated in 1932. It was the midst of the Depression, and with no money to go elsewhere, she was able to take one more year there, although it was a junior college. The following winter she stayed with friends in Sarasota, Florida, working as a waitress and attending two classes at the Ringling School of Art.

On July 18, 1934, she was married to Leslie Kohlman, whom she had met at Graceland College. They have lived in Houston, Texas; Tulsa, Oklahoma; Independence, Missouri; Guelph, Ontario; and since 1957, in Lamoni, Iowa. They have five children, eight grandchildren, and four great-grandchildren.

After moving to Lamoni, Aarona enrolled once more in Graceland College (now a four-year institution,) receiving her Bachelor of Arts degree with an English major. She became a professor of English at Graceland, and received her Masters degree from Iowa State University, Ames, Iowa. Her Masters thesis, *The Dialect of Grand Cayman*, was the basis for her book *Wotcha Say*. She is now retired as Professor Emerita.